POTATO COOKERY

BY
TOM HOGE

PAUL HARRIS PUBLISHING

EDINBURGH

First published in Great Britain 1980
by Paul Harris Publishing
25 London Street, Edinburgh

Manufactured in the United States of America
Originally published by Cornerstone Library, Inc.
a division of Simon & Schuster

ISBN 0-86228-014-1

Contents

BRITISH CONVERSION TABLE

British measures are larger than standard American measures which are as follows:

1 American Cup	= 8 fluid ounces
	= 4/5 of a B.S. cup
16 American tablespoons	= 1 American cup
3 American teaspoons	= 1 American tablespoon
	= 4/5 of a B.S. tablespoon
1 American pint	= 16 fluid ounces
	= 4/5 of an Imperial pint

TABLE OF HANDY WEIGHTS AND MEASURES

	approx. weight of 1 level cup
Flour	5 oz.
Sugar, caster or granulated	8 oz.
Sugar, demarara	7 oz.
Sugar, icing	5 oz.
Fresh breadcrumbs	3 oz.
Currants	8 oz.
Sultanas	6 oz.
Jam	14 oz.
Fat, dripping or margarine	¾-1 lb.
	8 oz.

Foreword

Potatoes, among the most ubiquitous and useful of vegetables, are pretty much taken for granted. Other vegetables enjoy intermittent vogues and have champions who praise them as an integral part of la nouvelle cuisine, or whatever cuisine happens to be trendy at the time. The potato is often dismissed as too pedestrian or proletarian, if not snubbed as fattening.

But now Tom Hoge gives proper honor to this protean vegetable which, as he reminds us, can be "both a staple for the needy and a delicacy for the gourmet."

When I read the galley proofs of *Potato Cookery* before publication, Hoge's many unusual recipes and his account of the travels and varying reception of the peripatetic potato struck a responsive culinary chord.

In our home, potatoes have long been welcome. In winter a simple baked potato is a special comfort. The burnished scent of crisping skins promises warmth and well-being, delightfully delivered by the juxtaposition of mealy, hot potato and melting butter.

In summer the potato stars as picnic fare. What would an alfresco meal be without a delectable potato salad, the waxy new potatoes tossed with an herb-enhanced vinaigrette, each ivory morsel filmed with good olive oil and vinegar, and enlivened with a tang of mustard—or one of the other potato salads of which Tom Hoge gives so inviting an assortment.

Potatoes in soups serve dual roles—as flavorers and natural thickeners, demonstrated in Hoge's suavely elegant vichyssoise and pumpkin-hued carrot and dill soup.

Tiny new potatoes make a beguiling cocktail nibble, boiled, stuffed with caviar—whether beluga of lofty reputation and price or the affordable kind—lumpfish or salmon roe, each mini morsel capped with a snowy coverlet of sour cream.

Hoge gives us versatile potato recipes in a multitude of guises: in a supporting role; as the main event, suitably dressed up or reinforced (as it often was before the turn of the century); in pancakes; as flour, in cookies, cakes and puddings. Or, and this will surprise many, as a diet food. He assures us that it's not the potato that adds the unwanted calories but the calorific concomitants. His chapter, "The Potato as a Diet Food," is a mine of low-caloried ways for our hero.

And, of course, potatoes are a staple in almost every ethnic cuisine. That storehouse of French gastronomic lore, *Larousse*, lists (by my count) 103 potato dishes—from Pommes de Terre Anna to Pommes de Terre Yvette. (Amusingly enough, Yvette is simply another name for Anna—perhaps I should reduce that count to 102.) Hoge's recipe for these delicious browned-in-butter potato cakes is excellent.

On the following pages Tom Hoge shows us that the plebeian potato can inspire an engagingly interesting book as well as fascinating fare for the table.

DORIS TOBIAS
Food and Wine Columnist
Women's Wear Daily and *W*

Introduction

If beef's the King of Meat,
Potato's the Queen of the Garden World.

Old Irish saying

If you ever visit the hamlet of Hirschorn in England's
Neckar Valley and climb the hill that leads to a romantic
old castle, you will find a quaint monument. On it is
written, "To God and Sir Francis Drake who brought to
Europe, for the everlasting benefit of the poor, the
potato."

The dedication should have included the affluent as
well as the indigent, for the spud has been both a staple
for the needy and a delicacy for the gourmet. Such popularity was a long time coming. The tuber originated in the
Western Hemisphere, where the Incas cultivated it as
early as 500 B.C. Sixteenth-century Spaniards carried it
back to Europe, where it was denounced by some as a
poison and an aphrodisiac and by others as unclean
because it reproduced by budding rather than by sexual
fertilization. Later, it became a fashionable vegetable in
Europe while still being considered inedible by Americans. However, in the fall of 1978, United States farmers
harvested 31.8 billion pounds of potatoes. The vegetable

has been honored with monuments, blessed by priests, and praised in legislation.

What has the potato got going for it to merit such plaudits after years of abuse? Take a twelve-ounce spud. It contains most of the vitamin C an adult needs each day, and its protein contains all the amino acids essential to nutrition. It provides thiamine, riboflavin, niacin, iron, calcium, and phosphorus. In addition, it contains no fat and only about 200 calories. According to one nutritionist, man can live on potatoes alone for almost five months and remain in good health.

The potato is also one of the cheapest vegetables available. For this reason, the United States Department of Agriculture has undertaken research to produce a tuber highly resistant to plant disease and possessing flavor and cooking qualities superior to the one produced as recently as a decade ago.

Today, over 90 billion potatoes of about 150 varieties are grown throughout the United States, but they fall under four main headings. The russet has a dry, mealy texture, netted skin, and shallow eyes. The long white has a firm texture, smooth skin, light tan color, and shallow eyes. The round red with its firm texture and smooth skin is marked by its color, whereas the round white is a creamy buff color, has a firm texture, and includes many varieties of different moisture content.

When buying potatoes, you do not have to be too choosy, but a few guidelines should be followed. Choose those that are fairly clean, firm, and smooth. Regular shapes can be peeled easily with little waste. It is also a good idea to buy potatoes of uniform size for even cooking. Avoid those that have wrinkled or wilted skins, soft, dark patches, cut surfaces, or a green appearance. If a potato has a soft core or feels soggy when pressure is applied to its sides, chances are it will be soggy when cooked. A musty odor produces a musty taste. However, potatoes do not have to be snow white—they are often ivory—but it is best to discard those of a decidedly yellow color.

Store potatoes in a humid (not wet), dark, and well-ventilated place. At the ideal temperature of forty-five to fifty degrees Fahrenheit, they will keep well for several weeks. At room temperature, they will begin to wilt at the end of a week, and those standing in temperatures of more than sixty degrees are apt to shrivel and sprout quickly. Do not expose potatoes to light for prolonged periods: they will turn green and have a bitter flavor. And do not refrigerate raw potatoes. At temperatures below forty degrees, starch will turn to sugar, and the potato will develop a sweet taste.

When preparing potatoes, gently scrub them with a vegetable brush or cellulose sponge. Leaving skins on them during cooking is an excellent way to conserve nutrients. Should you peel them, use a vegetable parer to keep peelings as thin as possible; some of the potato's nutrients lie close to the skin. Cooking them whole helps retain nutrients but also requires more cooking time.

To protect the whiteness of peeled potatoes when you leave them standing for a time before cooking, toss them with a little lemon juice. Soaking them in cold water can result in vitamin loss.

The ways of cooking a potato are legion. Here are some basic cooking instructions which you should know in order to prepare potatoes for the recipes included in this book.

To Boil

In a heavy saucepan with a tight-fitting lid, cook the potatoes in about 1 inch of boiling salted water until fork-tender (whole, 30 to 40 minutes; cut up, 20 to 25 minutes). (If the lid does not fit tightly, check occasionally to make sure the water has not boiled away. Add more water if necessary.)

To Rice

Prepare boiled or steamed potatoes; drain and peel. Force the potatoes through a potato ricer or food mill.

To Bake

Before placing in oven, pierce the skins in several places with the tines of a fork. This allows steam to escape, preventing the potatoes from bursting. If you prefer soft skins, rub the potatoes with a little salad oil. Place the potatoes on a cookie sheet or directly on oven racks. A medium-sized potato (about 5 to 6 ounces) will bake in 40 to 45 minutes at 400°F (preheated). However, baking temperatures can range from 325°F to 450°F (preheated). Adjust the time according to the temperature. Potatoes are ready when they are soft if pinched with mitted hands or tested with a thin skewer or fork.

To Steam

Steaming is an excellent way to preserve nutrients. Place a wire rack on the bottom of a kettle or large saucepan and add water to just below the level of the rack. (If a rack is not available, invert custard cups or crumple aluminum foil to make an elevated platform for potatoes.) Bring the water to a boil, add the potatoes, and cover the kettle tightly. Cook until fork-tender (whole, 30 to 45 minutes; cut up, 20 to 30 minutes). You may need to check the water level occasionally— add more if necessary.

To Mash

Prepare boiled or steamed potatoes; drain and peel. Using a potato masher, electric mixer, or ricer, mash the potatoes. Gradually add milk, salt and pepper to taste, and, if you like, butter or margarine. Beat until the potatoes are light and fluffy. The texture will depend on the amount of milk—the more milk, the creamier and thinner the potatoes.

To Pan Roast

Prepare boiled or steamed potatoes, but cook only 10 minutes; drain and peel. Arrange the potatoes in a shallow pan. Brush with melted butter or margarine or salad oil. Bake uncovered in a preheated 400°F oven 45 minutes or until fork-tender, turning occasionally and basting with more fat.

If roasting with meat, arrange peeled raw potatoes (halved or quartered) around meat in pan about 1½ hours before serving. Turn and baste with pan drippings to brown.

To French Fry

Peel and cut raw potatoes into strips about ¼ inch thick. Toss the strips into a bowl of ice and water to keep crisp and white while cutting the remainder. Don't soak. This lets the potato absorb water, prolonging cooking time and making the potatoes oily and soggy.

Pat strips dry with paper towels. Heat about 4 inches of salad oil to 390°F (using a frying thermometer to judge the temperature) in a deep-fat fryer or large, heavy saucepan. Place a layer of strips in a wire basket and immerse in hot fat, or place strips, a few at a time, directly into hot oil. Cook about 5 minutes or until golden brown and tender. Drain well on paper towels; salt lightly and keep warm in a 300°F oven until ready to serve.

The recipes included in this book will not all require fresh potatoes. There are few families in America who do not often enjoy frozen french fries or hashed browns, and potato flakes and granules have proved so tasty that the *Wall Street Journal* commented that home-mashed potatoes might someday become "as rare as homemade noodles." In each chapter, there are a few recipes that call for some form of prepared potatoes, and there are numerous ideas for dressing up frozen french fries.

POTATO COOKERY

1

THE POTATO
AS AN APPETIZER

One of the nicest things about that American tradition, the cocktail party, is the delicious assortment of appetizers and dips that highlight these affairs. The potato makes an appearance at more and more parties today, where guests are plied with crispy potato fingers, tangy puffs, and volcanic little mashed potato balls.

Potato Fingers

1 cup all-purpose flour
½ teaspoon salt
½ cup butter or margarine
3 cups mashed potatoes
1 egg yolk
1 teaspoon milk
Salt and pepper to taste
Grated Parmesan cheese

In a medium-sized bowl, mix the flour and salt. With a pastry blender or fork, blend the butter or margarine thoroughly into flour. Stir in mashed potatoes until well mixed. Cover and refrigerate the mixture at least 1 hour to chill. On a floured board with a floured rolling pin, roll out half of the potato dough about ⅛ inch thick. (The dough will be fairly soft. Keep the second half in the refrigerator until ready to roll it out.) Cut the dough into 3-inch by ½-inch strips. In a small cup, stir together the egg yolk and milk; brush the tops of the strips. Sprinkle with salt, pepper, and Parmesan cheese. Arrange the strips on cookie sheets. Bake in a preheated 350°F oven 20 minutes until golden brown.

MAKES ABOUT 4 DOZEN APPETIZERS.

As is now generally known, the potato did not originate in Ireland but in the high Andean valleys of South America, where the Indians developed the tuber. In this lofty land where corn does not grow well because of the cold, the potato has reigned supreme and continues to do so. And the variety is amazing. Indian markets in the mountains display a formidable assortment of potatoes. The skins of some are red and black, and their shapes vary from almost round to long and thin. Some are more solid than others and contain considerably less water than do most potatoes.

For many years, the Indians have employed a freeze-dried process of their own. The potatoes are turned into rocklike pellets, which keep for weeks and even months. After the potato harvest, the Indians carry much of their crop to ravines more than 13,000 feet above sea level and expose them to the freezing night air. The potatoes freeze at night, thaw under the sun, and freeze again the following night, until all moisture has left them and only rocklike pellets remain. These dried-out pebbles, known as *chuno*, look anything but edible. But after they are soaked a short while and then boiled, they turn back into tasty, edible potatoes.

Oriental Pick-Up Sticks

6 medium-sized potatoes, unpeeled
1 cup melted butter
¼ cup soy sauce
Crushed cornflakes
Sesame seeds

Scrub the potatoes. Cut each potato into 6 or 8 wedges lengthwise. Arrange on a baking sheet. Combine melted butter and soy sauce. Brush the mixture liberally over the potatoes. Sprinkle with crushed cornflakes and sesame seeds. Bake in a preheated 400°F oven 35 minutes or until crisp and lightly browned.

SERVES 6.

Balls of Fire

4 servings instant mashed potatoes
¼ teaspoon salt
20 drops Tabasco sauce
1 egg yolk, lightly beaten
2 tablespoons chopped green onion
1 tablespoon chopped parsley
1 tablespoon chopped pimiento
2 teaspoons Dijon mustard
⅓ cup grated Parmesan cheese
20 small squares Monterey Jack cheese
20 small canned green chilies
1 egg
1 tablespoon milk
¾ cup cereal flake crumbs
Oil for deep frying

Prepare instant mashed potatoes, reducing water by 2 tablespoons and adding an additional ¼ teaspoon salt. Stir in the Tabasco sauce, egg yolk, green onion, parsley, pimiento, mustard, and Parmesan cheese. Shape into tiny balls about 1 inch in diameter, alternately embedding a square of Monterey Jack cheese or a green chili in the center of each. Beat the egg with the milk. Dip the balls in the egg mixture and then roll them in the cereal flake crumbs. Heat the oil to 375°F and fry the balls a few at a time until golden brown, about 1 minute. Drain them on paper towels. If you prefer, bake the balls in a preheated 375°F oven until brown. Serve warm.

MAKES ABOUT 40 BALLS.

Italian Potato Puffs

1 small green pepper, seeded and
    chopped
1 medium-sized onion, chopped
4 tablespoons butter
4 cups mashed potatoes
4 tablespoons seasoned dry bread
    crumbs
1 package (8 ounces) mozzarella cheese,
    shredded

Sauté the green pepper and onion in 2 tablespoons of the butter until soft. Stir into the mashed potatoes in a medium-sized bowl. Grease 12 muffin cups evenly with the remaining 2 tablespoons butter. Sprinkle each cup with bread crumbs. Layer the potatoes and cheese in muffin cups with the potatoes on the bottom and top. Bake in a preheated 350°F oven 30 minutes, until the potatoes are golden. Turn the puffs out onto a platter. They will probably be moist and should be served like quiche on a small paper plate.

SERVES 12.

Potatoes Mayonnaise

3 medium-sized potatoes
2 tablespoons dairy sour cream
½ cup mayonnaise
Dash chili powder
Dash cayenne
Dash Tabasco sauce
Salt and pepper to taste

Boil the potatoes in their jackets, but do not overcook, since they must be firm. Let them cool. Peel and cut the potatoes into small cubes. Mix the remaining ingredients. Carefully coat cubes with mixture. Serve with toothpicks.

MAKES 3 TO 4 DOZEN.

Sausage Potato Rolls

1 pound country sausage links, cut into
    quarters
1 egg
2 cups mashed potatoes, instant
Salt and pepper to taste
¼ teaspoon Tabasco sauce
½ teaspoon Worcestershire sauce

Sauté the sausage quarters until brown and drain on paper towels. Beat the egg, add the potatoes and seasonings, and mix thoroughly. Place a spoonful of the potato mixture on a floured board and put a sausage bit on top. Roll so that the sausage is wrapped inside the potato mixture. Heat the sausage drippings (or vegetable oil if preferred) in a skillet and brown the rolls until slightly crisp. Serve with toothpicks.

MAKES ABOUT 30 TO 40 SAUSAGE ROLLS.

Tater-Stuffed Mushrooms

   1 pound large mushrooms
   ¾ cup mashed potatoes
   ¼ cup cottage cheese
   2 tablespoons dehydrated onion soup
       mix
   ½ teaspoon butter

Wash the mushrooms, removing stems. Set aside the tops and chop the stems. Combine the chopped stems with the remaining ingredients except the butter. Spoon into mushroom tops. Grease the bottom of a jelly-roll pan with butter. Arrange the mushrooms on the pan. Bake in a preheated 375°F oven 15 minutes, until bubbly and serve.

MAKES ABOUT 30 CAPS.

Miniature Party Cheese Wafers

   1 cup instant mashed potato flakes
   3 tablespoons sharp cheddar cheese
       spread
   2 tablespoons butter, melted
   2 tablespoons flour
   ½ teaspoon salt
   ¼ teaspoon paprika
   1 teaspoon cold water

Combine all ingredients, mixing well. Knead 2 minutes. Shape into 10-inch-long roll, about 1 inch in diameter. Wrap and refrigerate the mixture at least 2 hours. Slice thinly and bake on an ungreased cookie sheet in a preheated 425°F oven 10 minutes or until golden brown.

MAKES 36 WAFERS.

2

GLAMORIZING THE CHIP

One of the best ways to eat a succulent dip or spread is on a potato chip. Since its invention 125 years ago, the chip has become as basic to American tradition as apple pie.

In 1977, potato chip sales totaled about $2 billion, 40 percent of the $5-billion snack-food market in America. Outside the United States, chips are manufactured in thirty-nine countries, from Trinidad to Turkey.

Imaginative chefs have recently given the potato chip a larger role than afternoon snack or cocktail party dip scooper. They have devised recipes from pie crusts to stuffings in which chips play a star role.

The potato chip was originally known as the Saratoga Chip, and here hangs a tale. At Moon's Lake House in Saratoga Springs, New York, a fashionable nineteenth-century spa, a famous patron, Commodore Cornelius Vanderbilt, kept returning his order of french fries, complaining that they were not thin enough. Finally, in a fit of pique, the chef, George Crum, sliced some potatoes paper-thin, dropped them in bubbling oil, and dispatched them to Vanderbilt. Contrary to what Crum had hoped, Vanderbilt loved them.

The popularity of potato chips has increased each year and it is estimated today that Americans now annually consume about 4.5 pounds of chips per person.

Potato Surprise

8 medium sized potatoes, peeled and
  boiled
4 eggs, beaten
½ cup grated Romano cheese
½ teaspoon salt
  Dash Tabasco sauce
⅛ teaspoon cayenne
4 tablespoons butter
6 thin slices bologna
¾ cup diced mozzarella cheese
¼ cup potato chip crumbs

Mash the potatoes, add the eggs, grated cheese, salt, Tabasco sauce, cayenne, and 3 tablespoons of the butter. Grease a 9-inch-square baking pan. Line it with half of the chip crumbs. Pour over it one half of the potato mixture and cover with the bologna slices. Cover with mozzarella. Pour the other half of the potato mixture on top. Sprinkle with the remaining potato chip crumbs and dot with the rest of the butter. Bake in a preheated 300°F oven 40 minutes.

SERVES 8.

Potato Chip Pie Crust

1½ cups finely crushed potato chips
2 tablespoons melted butter

Mix the potato chip crumbs with the butter. Press firmly into an ungreased 9-inch pie pan or plate. Bake in a preheated 375°F oven 7 minutes. Let cool. This crust can be filled with any creamed seafood, creamed chicken, or creamed vegetables. Top with potato chip crumbs.

Stuffed Zucchini

    4 medium-sized zucchini
      Salted water
  ½ pound ground beef round
  ½ cup chopped chives
  ½ cup grated Romano cheese
  ½ cup crushed potato chips
    1 egg, beaten
  ¼ teaspoon Italian seasoning
    2 ounces dry sherry
    1 clove garlic, minced
  ¼ teaspoon paprika
      Paprika
      Salt and pepper to taste

Cook the zucchini whole in boiling salted water until done. Cut each in half lengthwise. Remove the pulp from the shells and mash well. Cook the ground round and chives in a skillet. Drain off any grease. Mix with the zucchini pulp. Add half of the Romano cheese, potato chips, egg, Italian seasoning, sherry, garlic, paprika, pepper, and salt. Fill the zucchini shells. Place in a baking dish, and sprinkle with the rest of the cheese and a little more paprika. Bake in a preheated 350°F oven 30 minutes.

SERVES 4 TO 6.

The largest single potato chip on record measured five by three inches. This report came from Reeds School, in Cobham, Surrey, England, on February 2, 1971. Mr. and Mrs. David Buja of Gardner, Massachusetts, reported a chip of the same dimensions on May 4, 1974.

Chips and Beans

1 can (about 1 pound) red kidney beans
1 cup chopped celery
¼ cup chopped onion
1 cup grated Swiss cheese
Salt and pepper to taste
¼ teaspoon Tabasco sauce
½ teaspoon Worcestershire sauce
½ teaspoon chili powder
½ cup mayonnaise
1 cup coarsely crushed potato chips

Drain the kidney beans and combine with the celery, onion, and cheese. Mix the salt, pepper, Tabasco sauce, Worcestershire sauce, and chili powder with the mayonnaise. Add to the bean mixture and toss lightly. Pour into a casserole and sprinkle with potato chips. Bake in a preheated 450°F oven 10 minutes.

SERVES 4.

Chips 'n' Cheese I

8 ounces potato chips (preferably thicker
    dip type)
½ cup sharp cheddar cheese, grated
½ teaspoon cayenne

Empty the chips onto a broiler pan. Sprinkle the chips with cheddar cheese and cayenne. Shuffle the chips to spread the cheese and cayenne. Place under the broiler until the chips become golden brown but not burned.

SERVES 4.

Chips 'n' Cheese II—for Casserole Topping

6 ounces potato chips (thin type)
4 ounces grated Romano cheese
1 teaspoon cayenne

Crush the chips and mix in a bag with the cheese and cayenne. Sprinkle atop whatever casserole you have cooked: meat, fowl, or vegetable. Place the casserole under the broiler a few minutes to melt the cheese and serve.

Meat Loaf With Chips

2 pounds lean beef, ground
½ pound pork, finely ground
½ pound veal, finely ground
½ teaspoon pepper
2 eggs, beaten
1 cup crushed potato chips
½ cup milk
¼ cup chopped onion
¼ cup chopped celery
¼ teaspoon allspice
1 tablespoon prepared mustard
4 slices bacon
Dry red wine, *optional*

Mix all the ingredients except the bacon and wine using your hands or a heavy-duty electric blender. Pack into a lightly greased loaf pan or form into loaf on a baking sheet. Top with bacon slices and bake in a preheated 350°F oven 1½ hours or until the loaf shrinks slightly from the sides of the loaf pan. If you like, baste the loaf every 10 minutes or so with dry red wine. Serve with a tomato or mushroom sauce if desired.

SERVES 8 TO 10.

Spicy Potato Chip Stuffing

1 tablespoon grated fresh onion
2 cups crushed potato chips
½ cup melted butter
Juice of ½ lime
1 ounce Cognac
¼ cup fresh parsley, chopped
½ teaspoon celery salt
¼ teaspoon garlic salt
Salt and pepper to taste

Cook the onion and crushed potato chips in butter until lightly browned. Mix in the remaining ingredients. Use as stuffing for fish.

MAKES ABOUT 3 CUPS.

Chestnut-Sausage-Chip Stuffing

4 dozen Italian chestnuts
2 tablespoons butter
1 small onion, minced
½ pound country sausage meat
2 teaspoons salt
¼ teaspoon pepper
Dash garlic powder
⅛ teaspoon sage
1 tablespoon chopped parsley
1 cup crushed potato chips

Cook and shell the chestnuts, mashing half and leaving the rest whole. Set aside. Melt the butter in a saucepan, add the onion, and cook 3 minutes. Add the sausage meat and cook 5 minutes, stirring when needed. Add the mashed chestnuts and mix well. Add the seasonings and crushed potato chips. Stir in the whole chestnuts.

MAKES ABOUT 4 CUPS.

Chips Mexican-Style

8 ounces potato chips
Juice of 1 lemon
Tabasco sauce to taste
Salt to taste
Worcestershire sauce to taste

Place the chips in a 2-quart bowl. Sprinkle the potato chips lightly with lemon juice, Tabasco sauce, salt, and Worcestershire sauce and toss lightly. Place on a cookie sheet and put in a preheated 300°F oven a few minutes until the ingredients sear into the chips, but do not burn.

Potato Chip Dips

Here are some dips that are good with the Saratoga chip. The first, Gladys Caviar Ball, was created by Mrs. Cornelius Vanderbilt Whitney, the great-great-grand-daughter-in-law of the old Commodore, who started it all the night he sent his french fries back to the kitchen. It is actually a spread.

GLADYS CAVIAR BALL

1 large-sized package (8 ounces) cream
    cheese
1 ounce heavy cream
½ teaspoon grated fresh onion
1 medium-sized jar lumpfish caviar

Mix the cream cheese with the cream to soften. Add the grated onion. Divide the cheese in half. In a shallow bowl, put a layer of cheese, then a layer of caviar, then the rest of cheese. Unmold, top with the rest of the caviar and frost sides with the cheese mixture. Serve with lemon wedges and spread on potato chips.

OYSTER DIP

1 large-sized package (8 ounces) cream
    cheese
1 teaspoon grated fresh onion
1 tablespoon chopped parsley
2 tablespoons dry sherry
1 tin drained smoked oysters, chopped
2 tablespoons heavy cream

Soften the cream cheese and mix with the onion, parsley, sherry, cream and oysters. Use as a dip with potato chips.

WATERCRESS DIP

1 large-sized package (8 ounces) cream
    cheese
½ cup finely chopped watercress
   Salt and pepper to taste
¼ cup heavy cream

Mix all ingredients together and serve as a dip with potato chips.

In May 1969, at Brisbane University in Australia, Paul G. Gully consumed 30 two-ounce bags of potato chips in 24 minutes and 33.6 seconds without drinking any liquid to wash them down.

3

POTATOES MAKE THE SOUP

No dinner is really complete without a soup to lead things off. In the summer, there are the chilled variety, like elegant Vichyssoise or velvety Green Goddess. Come winter, our thoughts turn to rich chowders, rib-sticking minestrones, and hearty cream soups. If we don't want something heavy, there are clear, tangy broths that can also warm our bones and put us in the mood for the meal to come. The potato is a key ingredient in all these and a good many other soups.

Vichyssoise

    1½ cups mashed potatoes, instant
    2 large leeks (white part only), chopped
        coarsely
    1 small onion, chopped coarsely
    2 cups chicken broth
    ½ teaspoon salt
      Freshly ground pepper
      Light cream

Prepare the potatoes according to the directions on the package and set aside. Cook the leeks and onion in chicken broth until tender. Pour into a blender and purée. Mix with the potatoes and seasonings and add the light cream to desired consistency. Serve chilled.

SERVES 4 TO 6.

Summer Squash Soup

Follow the directions for Vichyssoise, adding 1½ pounds diced crookneck squash to the pot containing the leeks, onion, and chicken broth.

SERVES 4 TO 6.

Lemon Broccoli Soup

Follow the directions for Vichyssoise, adding 1 pound fresh cut-up broccoli and ¼ cup lemon juice to the leeks, onion, and chicken broth.

SERVES 4 TO 6.

Grand Lady Potato Soup

by Jan G. Verdonkschot

Here is a soup for gourmets. The recipe was created by Dutch-born chef Jan G. Verdonkschot, who was named Chef of the Year in 1970.

2 tablespoons butter
4 leeks (white part only), cut into 1-inch bits
1 medium-sized onion, diced
5 medium-sized Idaho potatoes, cut into ½-inch pieces
4 cups hot water
2 teaspoons salt
2 cups hot milk

In a pot, melt 1 tablespoon of the butter and add the leeks and onion. Cook slowly for a few minutes, but do not brown. Stir with a wooden spoon and add the potatoes, water, and salt. Simmer the soup, uncovered, 30 to 40 minutes, until the potatoes are soft. Add the hot milk and the remaining butter. Taste the soup to correct the seasoning.

SERVES 6.

Carrot Dill Soup

Follow the directions for Vichyssoise, adding 3 large sliced carrots to the leeks, onion, and chicken broth. Also add ½ teaspoon dill weed to the seasonings.

SERVES 4 TO 6.

Caesar Soup

1 cup potatoes, unpeeled and thinly
   sliced
1 clove garlic, pressed
1 tablespoon olive oil
4 cups chicken broth
4 cups chopped romaine lettuce
3 anchovy fillets, rinsed
   Juice of ½ lemon
   Salt and pepper to taste
   Croutons
1 teaspoon Parmesan cheese

Cook the potatoes and garlic in olive oil in a saucepan over a low heat until the potatoes are limp. Add the chicken broth and chopped lettuce. Cover and simmer 15 minutes. Add the anchovies and lemon juice and simmer 2 to 3 minutes. Purée the mixture in a blender. Add salt and pepper. Serve chilled garnished with croutons and Parmesan cheese.

SERVES 4.

Green Goddess Soup

    1 cup potatoes, unpeeled and thinly
        sliced
    ½ medium-sized onion, sliced
    1 tablespoon butter
    2 cups chopped watercress
    2 cups chopped parsley
    1 can (4 ounces) water-packed artichoke
        hearts, chopped
    1 cup chicken broth
    1 teaspoon tarragon
    2 cups milk
      Salt and pepper to taste
      Watercress
  1½ dozen small cooked shrimp

In a saucepan, cook the potatoes and onion in butter until the onions are limp. Add the watercress, parsley, artichoke hearts, chicken broth, and tarragon. Cover and simmer 15 minutes. Add milk and simmer 1 minute. Purée the soup in a blender and add salt and pepper. Serve chilled garnished with watercress and shrimp.

SERVES 8.

When Alfred E. Smith finally spoke to his old friend Franklin D. Roosevelt in 1932, after the two had been estranged for several years, he said, "Hello Old Potato."

Salad Soup

1 cup potatoes, unpeeled and thinly
    sliced
1 cup chopped green onions
1 tablespoon butter
2 cups diced cucumber
2 cups shredded Bibb or Boston lettuce
3 cups chicken broth
1 teaspoon dill weed
1 carton (8 ounces) plain yogurt
  Salt and pepper to taste
  Sliced radishes

Cook the potatoes and onions in butter in a saucepan until the onions are limp. Add the cucumber, lettuce, broth, and dill. Cover and simmer 15 mintues. Stir in the yogurt and purée in a blender. Add salt and pepper. Serve chilled and garnished with radishes.

SERVES 4.

When the potato was finally accepted in Europe as a safe food to eat, Britain's Queen Elizabeth I decided to try some. Her reaction must have been dubious. No one thought to tell the royal chef what part of the plant was edible, so he served up the leaves.

Potato-Meatball Minestrone

    2 slices bread
    ½ cup evaporated milk
    ½ pound ground chuck
    ½ pound ground beef liver
    ¼ pound ground beef heart
    1 egg
    1 onion, finely chopped
    1 teaspoon salt
    ¼ teaspoon pepper
    3 cups water
    1 pound cut green beans
    2 cans (10½ ounces each) condensed
        beef broth
    1 pound medium-sized potatoes,
        unpeeled and cut into chunks
    ½ pound carrots, sliced
    ½ onion, coarsely chopped
    1 celery stalk, sliced
    ½ pound zucchini or yellow squash, sliced
    ¼ pound beet greens chopped
      Salt and pepper to taste

To make the meatball mixture, in a small bowl, soak bread in milk 5 minutes; then beat the mixture with a fork until blended. Add the meats, egg, onion, 1 teaspoon salt, and ¼ teaspoon pepper. Mix well. Set the meatball mixture aside. In a heavy Dutch oven with a tight-fitting lid, heat water to boiling. Add the green beans and reduce the heat. Simmer, covered, 10 minutes. Add the beef broth, potatoes, carrots, onion, and celery. Return to a simmer. Drop the meatball mixture by spoonfuls into simmering liquid. Cover and simmer 15 minutes. Add the zucchini, or yellow squash, and beet greens and cook, covered, 5 minutes more or until the vegetables and meatballs are done. Add salt and pepper.

SERVES 5 TO 6.

Soupe au Pistou

2 quarts chicken broth
3 medium-sized potatoes, peeled and cut
    into 1-inch pieces
½ pound green beans, cut up
3 carrots, sliced
1 medium-sized onion, chopped
1 tablespoon salt
¼ teaspoon pepper
½ pound zucchini, sliced
1 can (16 ounces) kidney beans, drained
4 cloves garlic, mashed
1 can (6 ounces) tomato paste
1 tablespoon dried basil
½ cup grated Parmesan cheese
½ cup chopped parsley
¼ cup olive oil

In a large pan combine the chicken broth, potatoes, green beans, carrots, onion, salt, and pepper. Bring to boil and simmer, covered, 10 minutes. Add the zucchini and kidney beans, simmer 10 minutes more, until all the vegetables are tender. To prepare the sauce, mix the garlic, tomato paste, basil, Parmesan cheese, and parsley. Gradually beat in the oil, a teaspoon at a time, until the sauce thickens. Just before serving the soup, stir in the sauce.

SERVES 8 TO 10.

Second-Day Soup

If you have 2 cups leftover green salad, a couple of boiled potatoes in your icebox, and an adventurous spirit, try this one.

2 cold boiled potatoes, peeled and sliced
3 tablespoons butter
3 cups chicken broth
2 cups leftover salad
½ tablespoon dill weed

In a saucepan, sauté the potatoes in butter until golden. Add the chicken broth and cook 15 minutes. Add the leftover salad, without draining off any dressing, and the dill. Simmer another 5 minutes. Pour the mixture into a blender and whirl a few minutes. Simmer another few minutes and serve.

SERVES 3 TO 4.

Potato Parings Broth

Peelings from 6 large potatoes
1 large onion, chopped
2 carrots, sliced
1 celery stalk, diced
½ cup green pepper, diced
1½ quarts water
1 spring parsley, coarsely chopped
¼ teaspoon Tabasco sauce
½ teaspoon Worcestershire sauce

Wash the potatoes thoroughly and then peel, taking off fairly thick strips. Put the parings and other vegetables into a pot with the water, parsley, Tabasco sauce, and Worcestershire sauce. Simmer 2 hours, until the vegetables are very soft, adding water as it evaporates. Keep tightly covered. Drain off the liquid through a sieve, season with salt and pepper, and serve hot.

SERVES 4 TO 6.

New England Clam Chowder

¾ cup chopped onion
1 tablespoon butter
2 cups potatoes, peeled and cubed
1 cup water
1 teaspoon salt
1 teaspoon bacon-flavored bits
  Dash pepper
2 cans (7 ounces each) minced clams
1 cup evaporated milk

In a large saucepan, cook the onion in butter until tender. Add the potatoes, water, salt, bacon-flavored bits, and pepper. Cover and simmer 30 minutes, until the potatoes are tender. Stir in the clams and evaporated milk. Heat but do not boil.

SERVES 6.

Potato-Cheese Soup I

12 small potatoes, peeled and sliced
6 cups chicken broth
1½ cups grated Swiss cheese
1 medium-sized onion, sliced
1 tablespoon chili powder
    Dash cayenne
½ teaspoon salt
¼ teaspoon pepper
1 teaspoon butter
1 teaspoon flour
1 cup heavy cream, scalded

Place all the ingredients except the butter, flour, and heavy cream in a saucepan, bring to a boil, and then reduce the heat and simmer until the potatoes are tender. Purée the soup in a blender. Bring the soup to a boil. Blend together the butter and flour and add this mixture to the soup a little at a time, stirring constantly. Cook the soup over a low heat 5 minutes. Stir in the scalded heavy cream and serve.

SERVES 6 TO 8.

Potato-Cheese Soup II

        2 cups potatoes, peeled and diced
        1 cup chopped onion
    ½ cup diced celery
    2½ cups boiling water
        ½ cup dry white wine
    2½ teaspoons salt
        ¼ cup butter
        ¼ cup all-purpose flour
        ¼ teaspoon pepper
        2 teaspoons Worcestershire sauce
        ⅛ teaspoon Tabasco sauce
        2 cups milk
        8 ounces sharp cheddar cheese, grated
        1 teaspoon minced parsley
        1 cup canned stewed tomatoes
        Pinch dill weed

Put the potatoes, onion, celery, water, and wine in a kettle with 1 teaspoon of the salt. Bring to a boil and simmer 15 minutes. In a saucepan, melt the butter, blend in the flour, and add the remaining salt, pepper, Worcestershire sauce, Tabasco sauce, and milk. Cook, stirring constantly, until smooth and thickened. Add the remaining ingredients and the potato mixture. Simmer a few minutes.

SERVES 6.

Potato and Carrot Soup

2 slices bacon, diced
1 onion, minced
3 cups diced potatoes
3 cups chicken broth
1 cup grated raw carrot
2 teaspoons salt
¼ teaspoon pepper
⅛ teaspoon Tabasco sauce
2 tablespoons all-purpose flour
3 cups milk

Cook the bacon in a kettle until golden brown. Remove the bacon from the kettle and crumble. Add the onion to the fat remaining in the kettle and cook until golden. Add the potatoes and chicken broth, cover, and simmer 15 minutes until the potatoes are tender. Add the carrot and seasonings. Blend the flour with ½ cup of the milk. Stir into the hot mixture and cook, stirring, until slightly thickened. Add the remaining milk and heat. Sprinkle with bacon.

SERVES 4.

Potato Soup Parmentier

4 leeks (white part only) finely chopped
3 tablespoons butter
4 medium-sized potatoes, peeled and
    diced
Water
Salt to taste
Dash Tabasco sauce
1 cup milk, scalded

1 ounce Cognac
1 egg yolk
   White bread, cut into squares and
      browned in butter

Brown the leeks lightly in 2 tablespoons of the butter. Put them in a covered pan with the potatoes. Add water to cover, salt, and Tabasco sauce. Cook on a medium heat until the vegetables are done. Pass the mixture through a food mill and add the milk and Cognac. Add enough water to make the soup the right consistency. Bring to a boil and then remove from the heat. Beat the egg yolk. Add a small amount of the soup to it, stirring constantly. Return the mixture to the pot. Mix well. Pour into serving bowls, adding 1 tablespoon butter and the bread squares.

SERVES 4.

Cucumber Potato Soup I

3 large cucumbers, pared
3 tablespoons butter
1 can (about 14 ounces) chicken broth
1 can (10¼ ounces) frozen condensed
   potato soup, thawed
2 ounces white wine
½ teaspoon salt
⅛ teaspoon cayenne
1 cup light cream

Quarter the cucumbers lengthwise, scoop out seeds, and dice. Sauté in the butter until soft. Pour the mixture into a blender, adding the chicken broth. Cover and beat until smooth. Pour back into a saucepan. Stir in the potato soup and wine. Add the salt, cayenne, and cream. Heat slowly to boiling.

SERVES 8.

Cucumber Potato Soup II

1 can (10¼ ounces) frozen condensed
    cream of potato soup
2 cups milk
1 ounce Cognac
    Dash Tabasco sauce
1 small cucumber, pared and diced
½ teaspoon salt
⅛ teaspoon pepper
2 tablespoons chopped parsley

Combine the soup and milk in a saucepan. Heat to boiling, stirring often. Remove the pan from the heat and stir in the Cognac, Tabasco sauce, cucumber, salt, and pepper. Simmer several minutes and serve with chopped parsley.

SERVES 4.

Potato Crab Bisque

1 can (10¼ ounces) frozen condensed cream of
    potato soup
2 cups milk
2 ounces dry white wine
1 teaspoon grated fresh onion
    Dash cayenne
⅛ teaspoon curry powder
1 can (about 3¼ ounces) crab meat,
    drained, boned, and flaked
1 teaspoon chopped chives

Combine the soup, milk, wine, onion, cayenne, and curry powder in a medium-sized pan. Heat to boiling over a medium heat, stirring often. Add the crab meat, simmer a few more minutes, and serve with chopped chives.

SERVES 4.

Potato Corn Chowder

1 can (10¼ ounces) condensed cream of
    potato soup
1 can (8 ounces) cream-style corn
1 cup evaporated milk
1 cup milk
1 tablespoon grated fresh onion
½ cup diced celery
1 teaspoon Worcestershire sauce
    Dash Tabasco sauce
1 teaspoon pepper
1 tablespoon chopped parsley

Combine all the ingredients except the parsley in a saucepan. Heat until bubbling. Serve with parsley sprinkled atop.

SERVES 4.

Potato Shrimp Soup Gratin

1 cup chopped onion
2 tablespoons butter
2 cans (10¼ ounces each) frozen
    condensed potato soup, thawed
3½ cups milk
1 teaspoon chili powder
½ cup diced green pepper
1 pound frozen raw shrimp, shelled and
    deveined
½ cup grated American cheese

Sauté the onion in butter until soft. Stir in the potato soup, milk, chili powder, and green pepper. Heat to a boil and simmer several minutes. Then add the frozen shrimp and heat to boiling again. Simmer 25 minutes, stirring several times, until the shrimp are tender. Before serving, add the grated cheese and stir until melted.

SERVES 6.

Oyster Chowder

1 pound small white potatoes, peeled
   and boiled
4 tablespoons butter
2 cans (10¼ ounces each) condensed
   oyster stew
1 can (16 ounces) green peas
1 can (12 or 16 ounces) whole-kernel
   corn
2 cups milk
3 ounces dry white wine
2 tablespoons instant minced onion
1 teaspoon salt
¼ teaspoon black pepper
1 teaspoon Worcestershire sauce
   Dash Tabasco sauce
   Chopped parsley

In a saucepan, sauté the potatoes in butter. Stir in all
the other ingredients except the parsley. Heat slowly to a
boil. Serve with chopped parsley atop.

SERVES 6.

Cod-Potato Chowder

2 pounds cod fillets
6 medium-sized potatoes, peeled and
   sliced
½ cup celery leaves, chopped
1 bay leaf
2½ teaspoons salt
   Dash cayenne
½ teaspoon chili powder
1 clove garlic, minced
4 whole cloves
3 medium-sized onions, sliced

½ cup butter or margarine
¼ teaspoon dill seed
¼ teaspoon white pepper
1 cup rosé wine
2 cups boiling water
2 cups light cream, scalded
Chopped parsley

Put all the ingredients except the cream and parsley in a 3-quart casserole. Cover and bake in a preheated 375°F oven 1 hour. Add the scalded light cream to the chowder. Serve the soup garnished with parsley.

MAKES ABOUT 2½ QUARTS.

Salt Cod Chowder

1 clove garlic, minced
2 shallots, chopped
6 medium-sized potatoes, peeled and
    diced
2 tablespoons peanut oil
4 tomatoes, peeled, seeded, and diced
2 quarts tomato juice
2 pounds salt cod, soaked overnight
¼ teaspoon sage
2 quarts water
2 ounces Cognac
Salt and pepper to taste

In a pan, fry the garlic, shallots, and potatoes in oil until lightly browned. Add the tomatoes and continue to cook until the vegetables are tender. Add the tomato juice, salt cod, sage, water, and Cognac and bring to a boil. Purée in a blender until smooth. Taste and season the chowder with salt and pepper. Reheat and serve.

SERVES 6 to 8.

Bonito Chowder

      1 tablespoon butter
      1 onion, minced
  1½ cups potatoes, peeled and diced
   ½ cup diced celery
      1 carrot, scraped and diced
      1 cup boiling water
      1 can (7 ounces) bonito—a saltwater fish
          related to the tuna family
      4 ounces white wine
      3 cups milk
        Dash Tabasco sauce
      1 teaspoon salt
   ¼ teaspoon pepper
        Dash powdered mace
      2 tablespoons all-purpose flour
        Chopped chives

Melt the butter in a large saucepan, add the onion, and cook until the onion is golden. Add the vegetables and water, cover, and cook 15 minutes, until the vegetables are tender. Add the bonito, white wine, 2¾ cups of the milk, and the seasonings. Heat the mixture well. Blend the remaining milk with the flour and add slowly to the hot mixture, stirring constantly. Cook the chowder until it is slightly thickened. Serve with a sprinkling of chives.

MAKES ABOUT 1½ QUARTS.

Seafood-Potato Chowder

1 pound small shrimp
Boiling water
6 slices bacon, diced
2 medium-sized onions, chopped
1 can (6 ounces) minced clams with
  liquid
2 medium-sized potatoes, peeled and
  diced
1 package (10 ounces) frozen succotash
3 tablespoons butter or margarine
3 tablespoons all-purpose flour
2 cans (10¼ ounces each) frozen oyster
  stew
3 cups milk
⅛ teaspoon Tabasco sauce
6 ounces lobster meat, cooked
1½ cups heavy cream
2 ounces Cognac
¼ teaspoon paprika
  Salt and pepper to taste

Cover the shrimp with boiling water and cook, reserving the liquid. Peel and devein the shrimp and set aside. In a large kettle, cook the bacon until crisp. Remove the bacon and pour off half the fat. Cook the onions in the remaining fat in the kettle 5 minutes. Combine the shrimp liquid and the liquid drained from the clams. Add enough water to make 4 cups. Add this liquid to the onions with the potatoes and succotash. Simmer about 15 minutes. Blend the flour and butter and add with the oyster stew and milk. Cook, stirring constantly, until the soup thickens. Add the remaining ingredients, including the shrimp and drained clams, and heat well.

MAKES ABOUT 2½ QUARTS.

Potato-Bean Chowder

    4 slices bacon, diced
    2 cups minced onions
    3 cups potatoes, peeled and diced
    2 cups Boston-style baked beans
    ½ teaspoon crumbled dried thyme
    2 cups water
    1 can (14½ ounces) evaporated milk,
        undiluted
      Dash Tabasco sauce
    ½ teaspoon chili powder
      Salt and pepper to taste
      Chopped parsley

Cook the bacon in a saucepan until crisp and remove. Add the onions and cook 5 minutes. Add the potatoes, beans, thyme, and water. Simmer about 15 minutes. Add the milk and seasonings except the parsley. Heat until very warm. Sprinkle the soup with bacon and parsley.

MAKES ABOUT 2 QUARTS.

Pepper Pot

1 pound honeycomb tripe, cut into 1-inch
   cubes
2 veal knuckles (about 1 pound each)
2 quarts water
2 bay leaves, crumbled
½ teaspoon marjoram
¼ teaspoon thyme
1 teaspoon basil
2 teaspoons salt
¼ teaspoon cayenne
1 cup chopped parsley
4 chicken bouillon cubes
1 medium-sized green pepper, diced
2 medium-sized onions, sliced
½ cup chopped celery
3 cups potatoes, peeled and cubed
8 ounces dry white wine
1½ cups milk
2 teaspoons peppercorns

Place the tripe and veal knuckles in a soup kettle or a large saucepan. Add the water, seasonings, and chicken bouillon cubes. Heat to boiling over a medium heat. Cook, covered, 10 minutes. Skim if necessary. Cover and simmer over a low heat for 3 hours. Remove the veal bones. Add the vegetables to the stock along with the white wine. Cover and simmer 40 minutes. Add the milk and peppercorns, crushed if desired. Simmer a few minutes longer and serve.

SERVES 8.

Canadian Potato Soup

>   5 cups chicken broth
>   4 medium-sized potatoes, diced
>   1 cup chopped parsley
>   1 medium-sized head romaine lettuce, chopped
>   ½ teaspoon salt
>   ¼ teaspoon pepper
>   2 ounces dry white wine
>   Dash Tabasco sauce
>   2 tablespoons butter
>   Minced parsley

Bring the broth to a boil. Add the potatoes, parsley, and lettuce. Season with salt and pepper and add the white wine and Tabasco sauce. Simmer, covered, 1 hour. Strain through a sieve or food mill. Stir in the butter. Heat the soup again and serve garnished with additional parsley.

MAKES ABOUT 2 QUARTS.

French Potato Soup

3 cups chicken broth
1 ounce Cognac
  Dash cayenne
3 cups milk
8 medium-sized potatoes, peeled and
    diced
½ cup fresh chervil, chopped
  Salt and pepper to taste
3 tablespoons butter

Combine the chicken broth, Cognac, cayenne, and milk in a saucepan. Add the potatoes and ⅓ cup of the chervil and cook until the potatoes are tender. Strain the mixture through a sieve or food mill or whirl in a blender. Return to the heat and simmer until hot. Season with salt and pepper. Stir in the butter. Sprinkle soup with the remaining chervil and serve very hot with toasted French bread.

MAKES ABOUT 2 QUARTS.

Beef and Vegetable Soup

2 cans (10½ ounces each) condensed
    beef bouillon
1 pound boneless chuck of beef, cubed
1 tablespoon salt
½ teaspoon pepper
1 bay leaf
2 quarts water
1 teaspoon Worcestershire sauce
   Dash Tabasco sauce
2 cups potatoes, peeled and diced
1 medium-sized onion, sliced
1 large carrot, diced
3 celery stalks, sliced
1 cup lima beans
1 cup corn
1 cup cut green beans
2½ cups canned tomatoes
1 medium-sized green pepper, diced
   Salt and pepper to taste

Put the bouillon, cubed meat, salt, pepper, bay leaf, and water in a large kettle. Bring to a boil and simmer, covered, 1 hour. Add the Worcestershire sauce and Tabasco sauce and stir. Add the vegetables, bring to a boil and simmer, covered, for another hour, until the meat is tender. Season the soup with salt and pepper.

MAKES ABOUT 2½ QUARTS.

Chicken Soup Parmentier

1 large onion, minced
3 cups raw potatoes, peeled and sliced
3 cups chicken broth
1 package (10 ounces) frozen peas
2 tablespoons butter
1½ cups light cream
¼ teaspoon poultry seasoning
   Dash Tabasco sauce
2 ounces dry white wine
   Salt and pepper to taste
2 cups chicken breast, cooked, skinned,
    and finely diced
   Paprika
   Chopped parsley
   Croutons, about 1 cup

Cook the onion and potatoes in broth about 20 minutes. Add the peas and cook 10 minutes longer. Add the butter, cream, poultry seasoning, Tabasco sauce, wine, salt, and pepper and cook about 5 more minutes. Add the diced chicken and serve with a sprinkling of paprika, parsley, and croutons.

MAKES ABOUT 2 QUARTS.

Credit for acceptance of the potato in France should be given, at least in part, to an eighteenth-century French pharmacist, Antoine-Auguste Parmentier, who had lived on a diet of tubers while a prisoner of the Prussians during the Seven-Year War. A botanist of sorts, he was anxious to inspire enthusiasm for the vegetable among his countrymen. First, he gave a formal dinner for such notables as Ben Franklin and agriculturist Antoine Lavoisier. The meal consisted entirely of potatoes prepared in various ingenious ways.

To interest the general populace was more difficult. Resorting to psychology, he whetted their curiosity by having his potato fields ostentatiously guarded during the day. He left them unsupervised at night, however, and it was not long before curious peasants began stealing Parmentier's potatoes to plant and eat.

Finally, the wily Frenchman glamorized the image of the potato by preparing attractive bouquets of potato blossoms for ladies at the Court. Queen Marie Antoinette even wore the blossoms in her hair. Soon the royal family served the potatoes at court banquets. Famous chefs began outdoing one another with epicurean dishes like Pommes Marguerite, Snow Potatoes with Sour Cream, and the potato and truffle delight marinated in champagne known as Salade Francillon.

Ukrainian Borsch

1 pound beef round, in one piece
8 cups beef bouillon
  Salt and pepper to taste
1 teaspoon Worcestershire sauce
1 bay leaf
2 tablespoons butter
1 onion, chopped
2 carrots, scraped and sliced
3 medium-sized beets, peeled and shredded
½ medium-sized head cabbage, shredded
1 tablespoon minced parsley
1 can (8 ounces) tomato juice
¼ cup fresh lemon juice
3 medium-sized potatoes, peeled and
   diced
Dairy sour cream

Place the beef and beef bouillon in a deep kettle. Add the salt, pepper, Worcestershire sauce, and bay leaf. Bring to a boil and skim. Simmer, covered, about 40 minutes. In another pan, melt the butter and sauté the onion, carrots, beets, cabbage, and parsley 3 minutes. Add the tomato juice and lemon juice and simmer over low heat 10 minutes. Add the vegetables to the beef and broth along with the potatoes. Simmer, covered, about 1 hour or until the meat is tender. Skim when needed. Correct the seasonings. Remove the beef to a platter, slice, and serve separately. Serve the soup with a dollop of sour cream atop each portion.

SERVES 6 TO 8.

4

POTATO SALAD DAYS

Many people tend to take the potato for granted, a necessary but somewhat bland accompaniment to the meat, fish, or fowl that will play the star role. But the spud emerges as something else where it appears in a cool, crisp, savory salad dressed with hard-cooked eggs, anchovies, olives, pickles, or a host of other tidbits or in a hot salad, like the famous German potato salad dressed with julienne strips of ham or tongue.

The salad per se can be served at almost any stage of the meal. But the heartier versions, especially the meat and potato combinations, can fill the bill as the main course. The potato salad can be glamorous often, but rib-sticking too.

Potato Salad with Jellied Vinaigrette

JELLIED VINAIGRETTE

1 tablespoon unflavored gelatin
3 tablespoons sugar
1 teaspoon salt
¼ teaspoon pepper
½ cup cold water
1¼ cups boiling water
2 tablespoons vinegar
Capers
Pimientos
Hard-cooked eggs, sliced

POTATO SALAD

3½ pounds potatoes, cooked and diced
1½ cups chopped celery
2 whole pimientos, chopped
1½ cups mayonnaise
1 cup Vinaigrette mixture
Salt and pepper to taste

Combine the gelatin, sugar, salt, pepper, and cold water in a pan. Add the boiling water and vinegar. Cool.

Mix the potatoes with the rest of the ingredients. To assemble the salad, pour a little of the remaining Vinaigrette mixture into the bottom of a 3-quart mold. Decorate with capers, pimientos, and egg slices. Chill until thick, but not firm. Carefully spoon the potato mixture into the mold. Chill several hours or overnight before unmolding.

MAKES 2½ QUARTS.

Stuffed Tomato-Potato Salad I

3 medium-sized potatoes (about 1
    pound)
Salted water

6 medium-sized tomatoes
3 hard-cooked eggs
1 can (13½ ounces) tomato aspic
1 tablespoon vinegar
2 teaspoons lemon juice
1 teaspoon prepared mustard
1 teaspoon horseradish
½ teaspoon basil
⅛ teaspoon garlic salt
4 green onions, sliced diagonally
Lettuce leaves

In a medium-sized saucepan, in 1 inch of salted water, cook the potatoes, covered, 25 minutes or until tender. Place potatoes in a bowl. Slice off the top of each tomato. Dice the tops and set aside. Hollow out the tomatoes, reserving the pulp. Refrigerate the tomato shells. Slice the hard-cooked eggs in half, lengthwise. Remove the yolks for use another day. In a small saucepan over a low heat, melt the aspic. Spoon some of the aspic into the center of each egg half. Cover and refrigerate to set. In a blender, combine the remaining aspic, tomato pulp, vinegar, lemon juice, mustard, horseradish, basil, and garlic salt. Blend a few seconds until smooth. Drain, peel, and cube the potatoes, then cover with the aspic mixture. Add the diced tomato tops and green onions (reserving a few for garnish) and toss. Refrigerate, covered, to chill and marinate. To serve, spoon the potato salad into the tomato shells. Garnish with green onion lettuce leaves.

SERVES 6.

Yogurt Potato Salad

1 cup plain yogurt
2 teaspoons prepared mustard
2 teaspoons horseradish
2 cups potatoes, peeled, cooked, and cubed
½ cup sliced celery
1 medium-sized cucumber, sliced
¼ cup sliced onion
1 tablespoon chopped chives

In a large bowl, combine the yogurt, mustard, and horseradish. Add the remaining ingredients. Toss to mix well. Refrigerate to chill.

SERVES 8.

Confetti Potato Salad

6 medium-sized potatoes, cubed
Water
Salt
¼ cup lemon juice
2 medium-sized onions, sliced
6 hard-cooked eggs, quartered
1 medium-sized green pepper, diced
¼ cup diced pimiento
1 tablespoon salt
Dash pepper

Cook potatoes in 1 inch lightly salted water to which 2 tablespoons of the lemon juice have been added. Cook 15 minutes until tender and drain. In a large serving bowl, combine the hot potatoes and remaining ingredients, including the rest of the lemon juice. Toss gently and chill.

SERVES 12.

Beefy Potato Salad

1 pound cooked lean beef round, well
    trimmed
3 tablespoons wine vinegar
2 tablespoons sherry
1 tablespoon catsup
½ teaspoon prepared mustard
2 medium-sized potatoes, peeled,
    cooked, and cubed
¼ cup sliced fresh mushrooms
¼ cup dairy sour cream
  Lettuce leaves

Cut the beef into ½-inch cubes. In a large bowl, combine the beef, vinegar, sherry, catsup, and mustard. Marinate in the refrigerator 2 hours, stirring occasionally. Add the potatoes, mushrooms, and sour cream. Toss gently. Chill and then serve on lettuce leaves.

SERVES 4.

Red Onion Potato Salad

6 medium-sized potatoes, peeled, cooked
    and sliced
1 cup sliced celery
1 cup thinly sliced red onion
⅓ cup chopped parsley
¼ cup Italian dressing
3 tablespoons wine vinegar
2 teaspoons salt
  Dash cayenne

In a large bowl, combine the hot potatoes with the remaining ingredients. Chill and serve.

SERVES 6.

Caesar Potato Salad

1 egg
¼ cup Italian dressing
¼ cup grated Romano cheese
1 tablespoon Worcestershire sauce
2 teaspoons prepared mustard
1 teaspoon salt
4 medium-sized potatoes, peeled,
    cooked, and cubed
4 pitted ripe olives, sliced

In a large bowl, beat with a wire whisk the egg, Italian dressing, Romano cheese, Worcestershire sauce, mustard, and salt until well blended. Add the potatoes and olives, toss well, and refrigerate.

SERVES 8.

The Germans have a popular jingle which says, "He who has money may eat oysters; he who has none must feed on potatoes."

Nevertheless, today the potato dominates much of Germany's fare from simple, robust meals to gourmet dishes. But that was not always the case. For many years, the Germans did not accept the tuber as being edible. But in the seventeenth-century, King Frederick William of Germany, in an attempt to combat a major food shortage, threatened to cut off the ears of any peasant who refused to plant them. His son carried on the tradition by distributing free seed to the people, and he enforced his edict to plant them by stationing armed troops in the fields.

Today, the Germans make a dazzling variety of potato dishes, from hot potato salad to crunchy dumplings. The Rhineland is the potato center, where the spud is cooked in more varieties than it is in central and northern Germany. One specialty, Heaven on Earth, is a mixture of potatoes and apples eaten with slices of fried blood sausage.

Hot German Potato Salad I

1 can (10¾ ounces) condensed cream of
    celery soup
2 tablespoons lemon juice
¼ cup water
4 medium-sized potatoes, peeled,
    cooked, and cubed
½ cup sliced celery
¼ cup chopped parsley
2 teaspoons salt
½ teaspoon sugar
   Dash pepper
1 tablespoon bacon-flavored bits

In a large saucepan, combine the soup, lemon juice,
and water. Heat, stirring occasionally. Add the remaining
ingredients except the bacon bits. Cook until heated
through, stirring constantly. Serve with bacon-bit topping.

SERVES 8.

Over the years the potato has served other purposes in
addition to being a food. One account reports that the
ancient Inca Indians measured units of time by how long it
took a potato to cook. Presumably, they used a uniform-
sized spud to do this. Potatoes have also been used to clean
wood and silver, darken hair, and supposedly whiten skin.
Folklore claims it will even remove wrinkles and stimulate
circulation.

Hot German Potato Salad II

2 pounds potatoes, boiled, peeled, and
    thinly sliced
¼ cup minced shallots
1 cup beef bouillon
2 ounces dry white wine
    Dash Tabasco sauce
1 teaspoon horseradish
    Salt and pepper to taste
⅓ cup mayonnaise
2 tablespoons Dijon mustard
½ cup julienne strips ham
¼ cup julienne strips dill pickle
1 tablespoon chopped parsley
1 tablespoon chopped chives

In a bowl combine the potatoes, still warm, and the shallots. Pour the bouillon, wine, Tabasco sauce, horseradish, salt, and pepper over the potato mixture. Let the potatoes marinate 30 minutes. Drain off any liquid not absorbed. Put the potatoes in a serving bowl and fold in the mayonnaise combined with the mustard. Dress the salad with the ham, pickle, parsley, and chives.

SERVES 6 TO 8.

French Potato Salad with Sour Cream

2 pounds potatoes, boiled, peeled, and
    cut into strips
2 cups julienne strips celery
1 cup tongue, cut into strips
2 tablespoons minced onion
2 tablespoons white wine vinegar
1 tablespoon lime juice
    Salt and pepper to taste
½ cup dairy sour cream
½ cup black olives, pitted and thinly
    sliced

In a bowl, combine the potatoes, celery, tongue, and onion. Sprinkle with the vinegar and lime juice. Add salt and pepper and toss. Add the sour cream and toss again. Garnish with black olive slices.

SERVES 6.

Pink Potato Salad

¾ cup dairy sour cream
3 tablespoons French dressing
1 tablespoon wine vinegar
1 teaspoon salt
1 teaspoon paprika
    Dash pepper
4 cups potatoes, peeled, cooked, and
    cubed
1 cup sliced celery
¼ cup chopped pimiento

In a blender combine the sour cream, French dressing, wine vinegar, salt, paprika, and pepper until fairly smooth. In a large bowl, combine the potatoes, celery, and pimiento. Toss with the sour cream mixture. Chill.

SERVES 10.

Stuffed Tomato-Potato Salad II

4 large tomatoes
1 medium-sized potato, peeled, cooked, and diced
1 medium-sized carrot, peeled and chopped
¼ cup cottage cheese
2 tablespoons chopped parsley
½ teaspoon salt

Cut the tomatoes into halves and scoop out the centers. Strain the pulp to remove excess liquid and set aside. Pat dry the insides of the tomato shells with paper towels. Combine the tomato pulp, potato, carrot, cottage cheese, parsley, and salt. Spoon the mixture into the tomato shells. Chill.

SERVES 8.

Gourmet Marcel Boulestin once said, "If there is a vegetable that is taken for granted, it is the humble potato."

Pennsylvania Dutch Potato Salad

6 slices bacon, cut into ½-inch pieces
1 medium-sized onion, minced
½ cup wine vinegar
4 tablespoons olive oil
  Salt and pepper to taste
  Dash cayenne
2 pounds potatoes, boiled, peeled, and
    thinly sliced
  Lettuce
3 hard-cooked eggs

Sauté bacon in a skillet with the minced onion until the onion is soft and golden. Add the wine vinegar, 2 tablespoons of the olive oil, salt, pepper, and cayenne. Simmer the mixture until it is hot. Put the warm potatoes in a bowl and pour the hot dressing over them. Add more salt and pepper to taste, and if the mixture is too dry, put in the remaining olive oil. Serve the salad warm on bed of lettuce and garnish with halves or quarters of hard-cooked eggs.

SERVES 6.

Potatoes are grown in all fifty states of America—about 1,152,400 acres in all.

Potato Salad with Herring

2 pounds small potatoes, boiled, peeled,
    and thinly sliced
1 onion, chopped
1 teaspoon minced garlic
4 herring fillets soaked, drained and cut into strips
1/3 cup olive oil
2 tablespoons cider vinegar
    Dash Tabasco sauce
    Salt and pepper to taste
    Chopped parsley

Put the potatoes, still warm, in a bowl, adding the onion and garlic. Add the herring strips. Pour olive oil, vinegar, Tabasco sauce, salt, and pepper over the potato mixture. Toss and garnish with parsley.

SERVES 4.

New England Potato Salad

2 pounds potatoes, boiled, peeled, and diced
1 cup green pepper, finely chopped
1/2 cup celery, finely chopped
1/2 cup onion, minced
2 tablespoons chopped parsley
2 tablespoons cider vinegar
    Salt and pepper to taste
    Dash Tabasco sauce
1 cup mayonnaise
3 hard-cooked eggs, sliced

Combine the potatoes, green pepper, celery, onion, 1 tablespoon of the parsley, vinegar, salt, pepper, and Tabasco sauce. Fold in the mayonnaise. Mix and garnish with the egg slices and remaining parsley.

SERVES 6.

Potato-Egg Salad

⅔ cup peanut oil
¼ cup cider vinegar
   Dash Tabasco sauce
 1 teaspoon horseradish
   Salt and pepper to taste
 6 hard-cooked eggs
 2 pounds potatoes, boiled, peeled, and
      thinly sliced
 2 tablespoons chopped chives
 1 tablespoon chopped green olives

In a bowl combine the oil, vinegar, Tabasco sauce, horseradish, salt, and pepper. Finely chop the egg yolks and pour into the oil mixture, mixing well. Put the potatoes in a bowl and pour the dressing over them. Add more salt and pepper to taste and toss. Garnish the salad with chopped whites of the hard-cooked eggs, chives, and olives.

SERVES 6.

Potato and Beet Salad

    ½ cup vegetable oil
    2 tablespoons cider vinegar
    1 tablespoon Cognac
      Dash cayenne
      Salt and pepper to taste
    2 pounds potatoes, boiled, peeled, and
        thinly sliced
    ¼ cup minced scallions
    ¾ cup cooked beets
    ¼ cup green pickle relish
    2 tablespoons chopped parsley

In a bowl combine the oil, vinegar, Cognac, cayenne, salt, and pepper. Put the potatoes in a bowl and toss them with the dressing. Add the scallions, beets, and relish. Toss the salad and garnish with parsley.

SERVES 4 TO 6.

Hot Mashed Potato Salad

    6 cups hot mashed potatoes
    ½ cup diced celery
    ½ cup diced green pepper
    ¾ cup mayonnaise salad dressing
    1 medium-sized onion, minced
    ¼ cup milk
    ¼ cup cider vinegar
    1 tablespoon chili powder
      Salt and pepper to taste
      Paprika

Mix well all the ingredients except the paprika. Garnish with paprika and serve hot.

SERVES 6.

Salade Lorraine

6 medium-sized potatoes, peeled, boiled,
    and sliced
2 cups light cream
1 teaspoon wine vinegar
1 tablespoon Cognac
1 tablespoon capers, chopped
    Dash English mustard
    Dash Tabasco sauce
    Salt and pepper to taste

Cool the potatoes and mix with the cream. Add all the other ingredients and mix well.

SERVES 4.

Frankfurter and Hot Potato Salad

3 tablespoons bacon fat
1½ tablespoons all-purpose flour
1 teaspoon salt
¼ teaspoon pepper
½ teaspoon English mustard
    Dash Tabasco sauce
½ cup water
⅓ cup cider vinegar
5 cups potatoes, peeled, cooked, and
    sliced
1 medium-sized onion, chopped
    Chopped parsley
8 frankfurters, sliced into rounds
    Vegetable oil

Heat the fat and add the flour and seasonings. Stir in the water and vinegar. Add the potatoes, onion, and parsley. Heat well. Brown the frankfurters slightly in a little vegetable oil. Arrange them on the salad.

SERVES 4.

Balalaika Salad

6 medium-sized potatoes, boiled and
    peeled
2 large beets, boiled
1 pound boneless roast veal
1 pound boneless baked ham
¼ pound Swiss cheese
¼ teaspoon parsley
¼ teaspoon chives
¼ teaspoon tarragon
   Salt and pepper to taste
⅛ teaspoon cayenne
2 cups mayonnaise
2 hard-cooked eggs, separated and
    yolks sieved

Dice the potatoes, beets, veal, ham, and cheese into ½-inch cubes. Add the parsley, chives, tarragon, salt, pepper, and cayenne. Toss well. Add the mayonnaise and toss again. Add the sieved egg yolks around the center of the salad. Place the egg whites around the edge of the bowl.

SERVES 4 TO 6.

Dutch Navy Salad

12 ounces cold lean roast beef
2 ounces pickled onions
2 ounces pickled gherkins
1 pound cold potatoes, boiled and peeled
1 medium-sized apple, peeled and cored
2 small beets, peeled and cooked
6 teaspoons mayonnaise
Salt and pepper to taste
1 ounce lemon juice
Small head iceberg lettuce
2 hard-cooked eggs, sliced
2 medium-sized tomatoes, sliced
Chopped parsley

Dice the beef, onions, gherkins, potatoes, apple, and beets. Mix them with the mayonnaise and season with salt, pepper, and lemon juice. Place the washed and drained lettuce leaves in a bowl and spoon the salad mixture on top. Decorate the salad with egg and tomato slices and chopped parsley.

Serves 4.

5

THE EGG AND POTATO COMBO

The egg produced by the diligent hen is an almost complete food. It has the added bonus of averaging only 72 calories—which may explain why Americans consume more than sixty billion of them a year, more than are consumed by any other nation. And now the potato is playing a role in making possible an ever-expanding menu of egg specialties.

Eggs and fried potatoes have long been a popular breakfast dish, and for many years that was about as far as the association went. But of late there has been a growing number of egg dishes in which the spud is a key ingredient. To name a few, we have potato omelets, potato soufflés, potato-egg cakes, and baked potatoes stuffed with various egg mixtures.

Half-Moon Omelet

2 cups potatoes, peeled and finely grated
½ cup grated onion
1 egg
¾ teaspoon salt
¼ teaspoon pepper
2 tablespoons flour
1 tablespoon chopped parsley
2 tablespoons oil

Drain the potatoes well on paper towels. Toss in a bowl with all the ingredients except the oil. Heat the oil in a 10- to 12-inch skillet. Spread the potato mixture over the bottom and fry slowly on one side. Fill half of the pancake with the Indian, Bolognese, or Chicken Liver fillings (see below). Fold the pancake as you would an omelet and cut into wedges.

SERVES 4.

INDIAN FILLING

¼ cup butter
1 cup diced green pepper
⅔ cup quartered cherry tomatoes
2 cups diced smoked ham
1 can (16 ounces) whole-kernel corn,
    drained
Salt and pepper to taste

Melt the butter. Add the remaining ingredients and cook over a low heat about 15 minutes, stirring occasionally.

MAKES ABOUT 4 CUPS.

BOLOGNESE FILLING

- 1 cup chopped onion
- 1 pound lean ground beef
- 2 tablespoons flour
- ¼ cup butter
- ¼ cup tomato paste
- ⅔ cup red wine
- 2 tablespoons sliced pimiento-stuffed olives
- 2 tablespoons grated Parmesan cheese
- ½ teaspoon thyme
- ½ teaspoon garlic powder
- Salt and pepper to taste

Sprinkle the onion and beef with flour and brown lightly in the butter. Add the remaining ingredients and cook over a low heat 25 to 30 minutes, stirring occasionally.

MAKES ABOUT 4 CUPS.

CHICKEN LIVER FILLING

- 1 cup chopped onion
- 1 pound chicken livers, cut up
- ⅓ cup butter
- 1 cup sliced mushrooms
- ⅓ cup light cream
- 1 tablespoon sherry
- 2 tablespoons chopped parsley
- Salt and pepper to taste

Cook the onion and livers in butter until brown. Add the remaining ingredients and cook over a low heat 25 to 30 minutes, stirring occasionally.

MAKES ABOUT 4 CUPS.

Oeuf Toupinel
by Maurice Chantreau

French-born Maurice Chantreau is executive chef at the Midnight Sun Restaurant, a famed gourmet eating establishment in Atlanta, Georgia. Holder of numerous culinary awards, he was named the best chef of France in 1967 and was named one of the outstanding chefs in the world in 1972.

4 Idaho potatoes
4 tablespoons heavy cream
8 eggs
1 pound fresh spinach, sautéed

MORNAY SAUCE
2 tablespoons flour
2 tablespoons butter, melted
1 cup milk, scalded
Pinch salt
Dash white pepper
Dash nutmeg
2 egg yolks
1 heaping tablespoon grated Parmesan cheese
1 heaping tablespoon grated Swiss cheese

Bake the potatoes 40 minutes in a preheated 375°F oven. Cut the potatoes in half lengthwise and remove the pulp, reserving the shells. Mash the pulp and mix with heavy cream. Fill the reserved potato skins half full.

To make the Mornay Sauce, mix the flour and melted butter in a saucepan. Add the milk and stir well. Add the salt, pepper, and nutmeg. Let boil a few minutes on a low heat. Remove from the heat and mix in the egg yolks and grated cheeses.

In each potato half, break in 1 egg and put the sautéed spinach around the egg. Pour 2 tablespoons Mornay Sauce over each potato half. Arrange the potatoes in a baking dish and place in a 400°F oven until brown.

SERVES 8.

Potato and Egg Bake

1 teaspoon butter
3 cups mashed potatoes
8 eggs
2 tablespoons grated cheddar cheese
2 teaspoons paprika
1 teaspoon salt
¼ teaspoon pepper

Grease a 9-inch-square baking pan with butter. Spread the potatoes in the bottom of the pan. Make 8 evenly spaced indentations in the potatoes and break an egg into each. Sprinkle the potatoes and eggs with cheese, paprika, salt, and pepper. Bake in a preheated 400°F oven 10 minutes until the eggs are set and the cheese melts.

SERVES 8.

Potato Omelet Olé

1 medium-sized potato, peeled and diced
⅓ cup minced onion
2 tablespoons diced green pepper
1 tablespoon butter
¼ cup catsup
½ teaspoon salt
Dash pepper
4 eggs, lightly beaten

In a nonstick skillet, sauté the potato, onion, and green pepper in butter 20 minutes, stirring occasionally until the potatoes and onion are tender and light brown. Stir in the catsup, salt, and pepper and cook, stirring, 3 more minutes. Pour the eggs into the skillet and cook until set. Loosen the edges and fold in half. Slide onto serving dish.

SERVES 2.

Potato Soufflé

3 tablespoons butter
3 tablespoons all-purpose flour
1 cup light cream
1 tablespoon chopped onion
  Dash garlic powder
  Dash Tabasco sauce
1 cup mashed potatoes
3 eggs, separated and beaten
  Salt and pepper

Melt the butter and blend in the flour. Add the cream and cook, stirring, until thickened. Add the onion, garlic powder, Tabasco sauce, and potatoes and heat, stirring. Quickly stir in the beaten egg yolks. Season and fold in the stiffly beaten egg whites. Pour into a 1½-quart soufflé dish or casserole and bake 30 minutes in a preheated 350°F oven, until puffed and firm.

SERVES 4.

Potato Puff

2 cups cold cooked potatoes, riced
2 tablespoons melted butter
⅓ cup hot milk
½ cup grated cheddar cheese
½ teaspoon salt
¼ teaspoon pepper
2 eggs, slightly beaten
⅛ teaspoon onion powder
  Dash Tabasco sauce

Add to the potatoes all the other ingredients and pour the mixture into a greased 1-quart casserole. Bake in a preheated 350°F oven 30 minutes or until set.

SERVES 4.

Potatoes Hungarian

½ cup butter
2 cups dairy sour cream
1½ teaspoon salt
¼ teaspoon pepper
⅛ teaspoon garlic powder
⅛ teaspoon cayenne
6 medium-sized potatoes, peeled, cooked, and sliced
4 hard-cooked eggs, sliced
1 cup fine, dry bread crumbs
Paprika

Melt the butter in a saucepan, add the sour cream and seasonings, and mix. Put the potatoes, eggs, sour cream mixture, and crumbs in layers in a shallow baking dish. Repeat, ending with crumbs. Sprinkle with paprika. Bake in a preheated 350°F oven about 30 minutes.

SERVES 6.

Hoppel Poppel

1 large onion, sliced
½ cup butter
8 medium-sized potatoes, cooked,
    peeled, and sliced
¼ cup minced green pepper
8 eggs
½ cup light cream
    Dash cayenne
    Dash Worcestershire sauce
1 teaspoon salt
½ teaspoon pepper

Sauté the onion in butter until golden brown. Add the potatoes and green pepper and sauté until the potatoes are golden. Beat the eggs with the cream, cayenne, Worcestershire sauce, salt, and pepper and pour over the potatoes. Cook, stirring, until the eggs set.

SERVES 6 TO 8.

Potato-Egg Cakes Italienne

1 cup mashed potatoes
1 cup all-purpose flour
3 teaspoons baking powder
1 medium-sized onion, finely chopped
½ cup grated Romano cheese
    Dash Tabasco sauce
2 eggs, slightly beaten
    Salt and pepper to taste
    Cooking oil

Mix all the ingredients except the oil. Shape into 3- by 1-inch rolls. Fry in 1 inch of hot oil until golden brown.

SERVES 4 TO 6.

Boules

2 cups cold mashed potatoes
2 cups potato flour
2 eggs, beaten
1 teaspoon grated Parmesan cheese
  Salt and paprika to taste
  Croutons
  Boiling salted water

Mix the potatoes and potato flour and blend well. Add the eggs, one at a time, and season with cheese, salt, and paprika. Form lemon-sized balls, putting 2 or 3 croutons into the center of each. Drop into a pot of strongly boiling salted water. Boules will rise when ready. Drain and serve with a beef stew.

SERVES 6 TO 8.

Luther Burbank, famed botanist and father of the noted russet potato, sold his discovery to a seedman, J. H. Gregory of Marblehead, Massachusetts, for a mere $150.

Vichy Potatoes

1 pound boiled potatoes, peeled, quartered, and cooked
2 ounces butter
¼ teaspoon salt
⅛ teaspoon pepper
Dash Tabasco sauce
Dash Worcestershire sauce
1 egg yolk
½ cup all-purpose flour
1 egg, beaten
1 cup fine bread crumbs
2 cups cooking oil

Let the potatoes dry 10 minutes in a warm oven. Mash, adding butter, salt, pepper, Tabasco sauce, and Worcestershire sauce and mix over a low heat, stirring until smooth. Remove from the heat, add egg yolk, and mix about 5 minutes in the top of a double boiler to retain heat. Form the potato mixture into ball-shaped croquettes about 1½ inches thick. Roll them in the flour, then in the beaten egg, and finally in the bread crumbs. Fry in deep oil heated to 375°F until very brown but not burned. Drain them on paper towels.

SERVES 6.

Egg-Cheese Potatoes

1 pound potatoes, peeled, quartered, and
    cooked
2 ounces butter
¼ teaspoon salt
⅛ teaspoon pepper
    Dash Tabasco sauce
    Dash Worcestershire sauce
1 egg yolk
½ pound Muenster cheese, cut into 12
    large cubes
1 egg, beaten
½ cup soft bread crumbs

Let the potatoes dry in a warm oven 10 minutes. Mash well, adding butter, salt, pepper, Tabasco sauce, and Worcestershire sauce and mix well over a low heat, stirring until smooth. Remove from the heat, add the egg yolk, and mix about 5 minutes in the top of a double boiler to retain heat. Grease with butter about a dozen 6-ounce custard cups. Fill with the potato mixture to within 1 inch of the top. Put 1 cube of cheese in the center of each, pressing down halfway. Brush with egg and sprinkle with bread crumbs. Bake in a preheated 425°F oven about 6 minutes. Serve hot.

SERVES 6.

Orange-Egg Potatoes

4 large baking potatoes, baked and
   halved lengthwise
4 tablespoons butter
3 tablespoons heavy cream
2 egg yolks
   Grated rind of 2 oranges
¼ teaspoon grated nutmeg
¼ teaspoon ground cinnamon
   Salt to taste
   Orange juice

Scoop out the pulp of the cooked potatoes, reserving the shells, and mash with butter, cream, egg yolks, orange rind, nutmeg, cinnamon, and salt. Add enough orange juice to make a soft purée. With a pastry tube, squeeze the purée into 6 of the potato shells and decorate with rosettes if desired. Bake the potatoes in a preheated 400°F oven until golden brown and serve.

SERVES 6.

Potatoes Soubise

6 medium-sized baking potatoes
4 tablespoons hot milk
2 tablespoons butter
2 egg yolks
  Salt
1 tablespoon chili powder
  Ground cinnamon to taste
1 cup Soubise sauce

SOUBISE SAUCE

2 tablespoons butter
2 tablespoons flour
  Salt and pepper to taste
1 cup chicken stock
⅓ cup milk
1 medium-sized onion, chopped and
    steamed in butter

Cut a lengthwise slice off the top of each potato and bake in a preheated 400°F oven until done.

To make the Soubise Sauce, combine the melted butter and flour in the top of a double boiler. Add the salt and pepper and chicken stock. Bring to a boil. Add the milk and onion and blend.

Scoop the potato pulp out of shells and mash with the hot milk, butter, egg yolks, salt, chili powder, and cinnamon. Fill the shells with the potato mixture. Make a depression in the center of each and fill with Soubise Sauce. Heat slightly in a preheated 350°F oven.

SERVES 6.

6

BOLSTERING THE STAFF OF LIFE

Man may not be able to live by bread alone, but he would be hard put to do without it. The origin of bread goes back to the unleavened discs made by primitive man. But the big breakthrough was made when the ancient Egyptians stumbled onto a leavening agent. Another milestone was passed when Europeans finally decided they could safely eat the potatoes they had been decorating their gardens with for a couple of centuries. They soon discovered, among other things, that the spud, grated or mashed, gave substance to bread, biscuits, and muffins. Experimenting further, they found that delicious pancakes and waffles could be made from potatoes and that spuds also gave a lift to stuffings.

Potato Rolls

4 small French sourdough or onion rolls
¼ cup melted butter
4 servings mashed potatoes, instant
½ cup dairy sour cream
½ teaspoon nutmeg
   Grated Parmesan cheese
   Paprika

Cut a hollow in the top of each roll. Brush with butter and brown under the broiler. Make mashed potatoes according to the instructions on the package, omitting the milk. Stir in the sour cream and nutmeg. Fill a pastry tube with the potato mixture and squirt onto the hollowed rolls. Sprinkle with Parmesan cheese and paprika. Bake in a preheated 375°F oven 15 minutes.

SERVES 4.

Idaho Potato Fritters

2 cups water
1 teaspoon salt
2 cups mashed potatoes
1 can (8¼ ounces) sliced carrots, drained
½ cup sifted flour
¼ teaspoon cayenne
½ teaspoon nutmeg
   Fat for frying

Bring the water and salt to a boil, remove from the heat, and stir in the potatoes. Combine with the remaining ingredients. Heat the fat to 375°F. Drop the batter from a teaspoon into the hot fat, frying 2 to 3 minutes. Drain the fritters on paper towels.

MAKES ABOUT 3½ DOZEN.

Country Potato Bread

    4 servings (4 ounces each) mashed
        potatoes, instant
    1 envelope granular yeast
    2 cups warm water
    2 teaspoons salt
    3 cups whole-wheat flour
    3 cups white flour

Prepare the potatoes according to the directions on the package. Stir the yeast in warm water until dissolved. Add to the potatoes with the salt. Gradually beat in the whole-wheat and white flour to make a firm dough. Turn out on a floured board and knead until smooth. Cover with a towel and set in a warm place to rise until the dough doubles in size, about 1½ hours. Punch down, knead briefly again, and shape in 2 or 3 loaves. Let the dough rise again until nearly double in bulk, about 45 minutes. Place on a greased cookie sheet. Bake in a preheated 350°F oven about an hour, until the loaves are well browned and sound hollow when tapped. For variety, follow the recipe as given, but use all whole-wheat or all white flour; add 1 tablespoon caraway or cumin seed for flavor.

MAKES 2 TO 3 LOAVES.

Potato Pudding Puffs

    3 medium-sized raw potatoes, diced
    ½ cup water
    1 egg
    1 small onion, diced
    ½ teaspoon salt
    ¼ teaspoon baking powder
    Dash pepper

In an electric blender set on "grate," blend the potatoes with the water for a few seconds. Pour into a fine strainer, pressing the potatoes against sides with the back of a spoon to drain off all possible liquid. Return the potatoes to the blender and add the remaining ingredients. Blend at a low speed a few seconds. Spoon into 9 small nonstick muffin cups, filling each ⅔ full. Bake in a preheated 350°F oven 45 minutes.

MAKES 9 PUFFS.

When one thinks of Italy, the land of pasta, one rarely thinks of the potato, but even there it has played a role. In fact, the Italians were the first Europeans to promote the spud in stews and croquettes.

When a specimen potato was presented to Pope Clemente VII in the sixteenth century, he asked botanist Charles l'Escluse to define it. The latter said the vegetable was a "small truffle," and for several centuries the Italians referred to potatoes as *tartufoli*. Only in modern times did they begin to call it by the name *patate*.

The potato was grown in Italian gardens for many years as an ornamental plant. And even when it was declared edible throughout the rest of Europe, the Italians leaned heavily on pasta for their starch.

Then Italian cooks began experimenting with the tuber, using it in croquettes and ragouts. Finally, they concentrated on gnocchi made with potatoes and ravioli made from potato flour.

Potato Dumplings for Stew

2 cups mashed potatoes
1 egg
¼ cup flour
1 tablespoon minced onion
1 tablespoon chopped parsley
½ teaspoon salt

Combine all the ingredients in a small bowl, mixing well. Drop by heaping tablespoonfuls on top of a hot stew. Cover and simmer 20 minutes

MAKES 12 DUMPLINGS.

Potato Biscuits

¾ cup flour
1 tablespoon baking powder
1 teaspoon salt
1 tablespoon butter, thinly shaved
1 medium-sized potato, peeled, cooked,
    and mashed
6 tablespoons milk

In a large bowl, stir together the flour, baking powder, and salt. Add the butter. Stir in the potato and then the milk, blending lightly with a fork. Spoon into 12 mounds on a nonstick cookie sheet. Bake in a preheated 400°F oven 15 to 20 minutes, until golden brown.

MAKES 12 BISCUITS.

Potato Waffles

1 cup flour
1/3 cup instant mashed potato flakes
2 teaspoons sugar
2 teaspoons baking powder
1/2 teaspoon salt
2 eggs
1 1/2 cups milk
1 tablespoon salad oil

In a large bowl, mix with a fork the flour, potato flakes, sugar, baking powder, and salt. In a small bowl, beat together the eggs, milk, and oil and add to the dry ingredients, mixing well. Bake the batter on a waffle iron until golden brown.

MAKES 16 SMALL WAFFLES.

Mashed Potato Stuffing

3 medium-sized potatoes, peeled,
    cooked, and mashed
1 tablespoon butter, melted
1 medium onion, minced
2 tablespoons chopped parsley
1 teaspoon salt
Dash pepper
Dash garlic powder

Combine all the ingredients in a large bowl and mix well. Use to stuff chicken, turkey, or boned leg of lamb roast. Or place in a nonstick baking dish and bake in a preheated 375°F oven 40 minutes.

MAKES 2 1/2 CUPS.

Minty Apple Stuffing

　2 medium-sized potatoes, peeled, cooked, and diced
　1 cup diced raw apple
　¼ cup diced celery
　1 tablespoon butter
　1 teaspoon crushed mint leaves
　1 teaspoon salt

Combine all the ingredients in a large bowl and mix well. Use to stuff chicken, turkey, or boned leg of lamb roast. Or place in a nonstick baking dish and bake in a preheated 375°F oven 40 minutes

MAKES 2½ CUPS.

Rye Bread

　1 cup molasses
　4 cups warm water
　2 packages active dry yeast
　⅔ cup cooking oil
　2 tablespoons salt
　4 egg yolks
　2 cups hot mashed potatoes
　2 cups nonfat dry milk solids
　1 tablespoon caraway seeds
　2 cups rye meal
　7 cups dark rye flour
　4 cups all-purpose flour

In large bread bowl, add the molasses to the warm water. Crumble the yeast over this and let stand 10 minutes. Beat ½ cup of the oil, salt, egg yolks, and potatoes together and add to the yeast mixture. Mix in the dry ingredients. The dough should be stiff enough to pull from the spoon after it has been beaten. Add more white flour if needed. Brush the top lightly with the remaining oil and let it rise until it doubles in bulk. Punch down and let rise again. Punch down before shaping into 4 round loaves. Put loaves into 4 well-greased, 2-quart, heat-proof glass casseroles. Let the loaves rise until they are double in size. Bake in a preheated 400°F oven 15 minutes. Reduce the heat to 350°F and bake 40 minutes more.

MAKES 4 LOAVES.

Crown Center Potato Pancakes
by Beat Richei

Beat Richei, executive chef at the Crown Center Hotel in Kansas City, Missouri, was born in Berne, Switzerland, and apprenticed at a hotel in Zurich. He was formerly executive chef at the Dusit-Thani Hotel in Bangkok, Thailand.

10 large Idaho potatoes, peeled and diced
 2 carrots, scraped and sliced
 1 onion, peeled and chopped
 4 tablespoons melted butter
 3 eggs, beaten
 1 cup flour
   Pinch nutmeg
 ½ teaspoon salt
 ¼ teaspoon white pepper
 1 teaspoon baking powder
 3 ounces vegetable oil
   Chopped fresh chives and bacon bits, about 1 cup
30 slices Canadian bacon
 3 cups applesauce

Grind the potatoes, carrots, and onion through the medium blade in a meat chopper. Drain. Add the butter, eggs, flour, nutmeg, salt, pepper, and baking powder and mix well. On a floured board, make small patties about ½ inch thick. In a shallow pan, fry the patties in 2 inches of oil heated to 375°F. Turn and cook until the potatoes are done and golden brown. Garnish with chives and bacon bits. Serve 3 slices Canadian bacon and 2 ounces applesauce with each portion.

SERVES 10.

Potato-Pumpernickel Bread

1½ cups cold water
¾ cup yellow corn meal
1½ cups boiling water
1½ teaspoons salt
2 tablespoons honey
2 tablespoons shortening
2 packages active dry yeast
¼ cup very warm water
2 cups cooked potatoes, peeled and riced
4 cups rye flour
4 cups whole-wheat flour

Stir the cold water into the corn meal in a saucepan. Add the boiling water and cook, stirring constantly, until thick. Add salt, honey, and shortening and let stand until lukewarm. Crumble the yeast into the very warm water, let stand a few minutes, and then stir until dissolved. Add the yeast and riced potatoes to the corn meal mixture, mixing well. Stir in the flours. Turn out on a floured pastry board and knead the dough until it is smooth and satiny. Place in a greased bowl, turn once, cover, and let rise until double in bulk. Divide the dough into 3 portions, form into balls, and let rest a few minutes. Roll each portion twice as long and twice as wide as the pan in which it is to be baked. Fold ends into the center and overlap slightly. Press the sides to seal and fold over in a similar fashion to fit the pan. Put each loaf in a greased pan with the seam side down. Let it rise until its size doubles. Bake in a preheated 375°F oven about 1 hour.

MAKES 3 LOAVES.

Tyrolian Potato Bladl
by Peter Schott

Austrian-born Peter Schott is executive chef at Sun Valley Lodge, the famed winter and summer Idaho resort. Before coming to America, he worked as a chef at various hotels in Austria and Switzerland.

      4 medium-sized Idaho potatoes
    ⅔ stick of butter
    ½ cup water
      2 teaspoons salt
    ½ teaspoon white pepper
    1⅓ cups flour
      Vegetable oil for deep-fat frying

Cook the potatoes unpeeled and store in the refrigerator overnight. Slowly heat the butter and water together until the butter melts. Peel the potatoes and grate on a fine grater. Arrange the grated potatoes on a table and create an opening in the center. Pour the lukewarm water and butter combination into the opening and add the salt and pepper. Toss the dough together until the liquid is absorbed and then add the flour. Work the dough together until it can be gathered into a compact ball. On a lightly floured surface, knead the dough quickly, pressing it forward and folding it back on itself, until the dough is smooth. Gather the dough into a ball, drape a kitchen towel over the top, and let it rest 15 minutes. Pour the vegetable oil into a deep frying pan to the depth of about 3 inches and heat it until it reaches 400°F on a frying thermometer. Divide the dough into 6 equal parts. Roll out each part on the floured surface to about a ⅛-inch thickness and cut into 3-inch squares. Fry each square on both sides and transfer to paper towels to drain while the rest are being fried.

SERVES 6.

White Potato Bread

½ cup butter
1½ cups potatoes, peeled, cooked, and
      riced
2 tablespoons honey
2 teaspoons salt
1 cup milk, scalded
2 packages active dry yeast
⅓ cup very warm water
5½ cups sifted all-purpose flour
1 egg white
1 tablespoon water

Add the butter to the hot potatoes and stir until melted. Add the honey, salt, and milk. Sprinkle or crumble the yeast into the water and let stand a few minutes until the yeast dissolves. Add the yeast to the milk mixture. Stir in 3 cups of the flour and beat until smooth. Gradually stir in enough of the remaining flour to make a firm dough. Knead for 10 minutes. Put the dough in a greased bowl, cover, and let rise until double in bulk. Punch down and let rise again. Punch the dough down and shape it into 1 large or 2 smaller braids and put on a greased cookie sheet. Cover and let rise. Slightly beat the egg white with the water and brush the bread with it. Bake in a preheated 400°F oven 10 minutes. Lower the heat to 350°F and bake 35 minutes longer.

MAKES 1 TO 2 LOAVES.

Potato Rolls

    1 package active dry yeast
    1 cup very warm water
    2 eggs
    ⅓ cup honey
    1 tablespoon salt
    1 cup cooking oil
    1½ cups warm potatoes, peeled, cooked,
        and riced
    ½ cup nonfat dry milk solids
    4½ to 5 cups sifted all-purpose flour
    1 egg white
    1 tablespoon water
    Sesame seeds

Crumble the yeast into the water. Let stand 10 minutes and then stir until dissolved. Into the large bowl of an electric mixer put the eggs, honey, salt, ⅓ cup of the oil, potatoes, milk solids, and yeast mixture. Beat at a low speed until well blended. Gradually add 2 cups of the flour and beat well. Add enough of the remaining flour, mixing by hand, so that the dough forms a ball away from the sides of the bowl. Let the dough rise until it doubles in size. Roll the dough out on a floured board until it is about 1½ inches thick. To shape the rolls, cut the dough with a floured 2¼-inch biscuit cutter. Roll the edges of each roll lightly in the remaining oil and put them into a baking pan (13- by 9- by 2-inches). Allow them to rise again. Slightly beat the egg white with the water and brush the rolls with it. Sprinkle them heavily with sesame seeds. Bake in a preheated 400°F oven about 25 minutes.

MAKES ABOUT 20 ROLLS.

Potato Beignets

½ cup water
⅓ cup butter or margarine
½ cup flour
1 egg
¾ teaspoon salt
¼ teaspoon cinnamon
Pinch mace
1¾ cups mashed Idaho potatoes (about 2
large)
Fat for deep frying

In a medium-sized saucepan over a high heat bring the water to boiling. Reduce the heat to low and add the butter and flour, stirring constantly, until mixture forms a ball. Remove from the heat and allow to cool. Beat in the egg, salt, cinnamon, and mace until smooth. Add the mashed potatoes and mix thoroughly. Cover and chill several hours. Drop the batter by heaping tablespoons into deep fat heated to 375°F. Fry about 3 to 4 minutes on each side, until golden brown. Drain on absorbent paper.

SERVES 4 TO 6.

Potato Doughnuts

2 eggs
1 cup honey
2 tablespoons melted butter
1 cup mashed potatoes
1 cup buttermilk
4½ cups all-purpose flour
4 teaspoons baking powder
1 teaspoon baking soda
1 teaspoon salt
½ teaspoon powdered mace
½ teaspoon ground ginger.
Fat for deep frying
Sugar, optional

In a bowl, beat the eggs with the honey. Stir in the melted butter, mashed potatoes, and buttermilk. Sift the flour with the baking powder, baking soda, salt, mace, and ginger. Add the dry ingredients to egg mixture and blend. Chill the dough 1 to 2 hours. Roll the dough out to a ½-inch thickness. Cut into rounds with a doughnut cutter or glass. Fry in fat heated to 365°F a few minutes on each side, until light brown. Drain them on paper towels. Dust with sugar if desired.

MAKES ABOUT 4 DOZEN.

Potato Pancakes

    6 medium-sized potatoes
    2 eggs
    1 small onion, grated
 1½ teaspoons salt
    ¼ teaspoon pepper
    ¼ teaspoon paprika
    ⅛ teaspoon powdered mace
    1 tablespoon all-purpose flour
    Vegetable shortening

Pare and shred the potatoes, making about 3 cups. If the potatoes are shredded ahead of time, place them in a bowl and cover with cold water until the pancakes are to be mixed; then drain the potatoes and dry well with paper towels. Beat the eggs in a large bowl and stir in the potatoes, onion, salt, pepper, paprika, and powdered mace. Sprinkle the flour over the top and stir in. Melt enough shortening in a large heavy frying pan to make a depth of ¼ inch and heat. Drop the potato mixture, ¼ cup for each cake, into the hot shortening, flattening slightly with the back of a spoon. Fry slowly, turning once, about 5 minutes, until crisp and golden. Serve hot.

SERVES 8.

Potato Bow-Tie Doughnuts

1 cup potatoes, peeled, cooked, and riced
1 cup water used to cook potatoes
1 cup milk
½ cup butter or margarine
½ teaspoon salt
1 cup sugar
2 packages active dry yeast
¼ cup warm water
3 eggs, well beaten
1 teaspoon cinnamon
1 teaspoon ground nutmeg
8 cups unsifted all-purpose flour
   Vegetable oil for frying
   Confectioners' sugar

In a saucepan, heat the potato water and milk almost to boiling. Pour into a large bowl and add the butter or margarine, salt, sugar, and riced potatoes. Cool to lukewarm. Sprinkle the yeast over the warm water in a small cup. Let stand 5 minutes. Add the yeast to the potato mixture along with the eggs. Add the spices. Beat in the flour to make a soft dough. Turn the dough into a greased bowl and cover. Let rise in a warm place until double in bulk. This will take about 2 hours. Punch down the dough and roll out ¼ inch thick on a floured board. Cut with a 3-inch round cutter and twist to make bow ties. Place bow ties on a floured baking sheet and let rise until their size doubles. Put enough oil in a large saucepan to make a depth of 3 to 4 inches and heat to 375°F. Add 3 or 4 doughnuts at a time and cook, turning once, 2 or 3 minutes, until golden brown. Drain on paper towels. Serve warm or cool, sprinkled with confectioners' sugar.

MAKES ABOUT 5 DOZEN DOUGHNUTS.

Potato-Carrot Pancakes

1½ cups potatoes, peeled, and coarsely
    shredded
1½ cups carrots, scraped and coarsely
    shredded
  2 tablespoons flour
  3 tablespoons wheat germ
 ½ teaspoon salt
  2 tablespoons sugar
 ¼ teaspoon cinnamon
  4 eggs, slightly beaten
  2 tablespoons butter or margarine
    Honey or maple syrup

In a large bowl, combine the potatoes and carrots. Sprinkle the mixture with flour and toss well. Stir in the remaining ingredients, except the butter or margarine. Melt 1 tablespoon of the butter or margarine in a large skillet. Use ¼ cup of the batter for each pancake. Spoon onto the skillet, flatten, and cook 5 minutes. Turn and cook 5 minutes longer until golden brown. Repeat with the remaining batter, adding the remaining butter or margarine as needed. Serve with honey or maple syrup.

MAKES 12 PANCAKES.

7

FLOUR FROM POTATOES

In addition to its many other roles, the potato has long served as a finely sifted flour that is still used extensively in many parts of Europe and Israel. The potatoes are ground to a pulp and freed from their fibers. The residue is a flour or starch.

Often substituted for cornstarch, potato flour is still used in Old World and some American kitchens for making gravies and sauces. It is also used for thickening stewed fruits in puddings or cold soups and for baking, since it gives cakes a dry texture.

When making delicate gravies and sauces, many cooks find potato flour preferable to cornstarch as a thickener, since it does not transmit a raw flavor even when cooked only for a short time.

In fruit puddings, potato flour gives the dish an attractive, clear appearance. However, when it is boiled, potato flour tends to thin out, and sauces thickened with it should be served at once.

It should also be borne in mind that potato flour does not have the same thickening power as regular flour. If you substitute potato flour in a recipe, remember that one and a half teaspoons of potato flour equal one teaspoon all-purpose flour. On the other hand, potato flour can generally be substituted for cornstarch in equal amounts.

Potato flour tends to deteriorate more quickly than cornstarch and should not be kept on hand for more than three or four weeks. This is probably one reason it is not used more extensively in America.

You may have trouble finding potato flour in supermarkets, but try shops that serve customers of German or Scandinavian extraction. Potato flour can also be found in kosher stores during Passover, when it is used instead of regular flour.

Wine-Cheese Soup

1½ cups potato flour
½ onion, finely chopped
1 cup dry red wine
3 cups cold water
5 cups beef bouillon
   Salt and pepper to taste
2 slices white bread
   Butter
4 tablespoons grated Swiss cheese

Put the flour in a skillet and stir steadily over a low heat until golden brown. In a pot, combine the onion and wine and reduce over heat to half volume. Mix the cold water with the browned flour until smooth. Add the flour mixture to the wine and onion along with the beef bouillon, salt, and pepper and simmer 45 minutes. Cut the white bread into small cubes and sauté until golden brown. Strain the soup into individual bowls. Sprinkle each bowl with 1 tablespoon Swiss cheese and ¼ of the croutons.

SERVES 4.

Gooseberry Soup

3 cups gooseberries
6 cups water
  Grated rind of 1 lemon
2 tablespoons lemon juice
1 cup sugar or more to taste
1 tablespoon potato flour
  Water
  Whipped cream

Cook the gooseberries in the water with the lemon rind until soft. Mix in a blender until smooth. Add the lemon juice, sugar, and potato flour, dissolved in a little water, and mix. Heat in a pot until the soup thickens. Cool before serving. This soup is served as a first course in Scandinavia, but it is also good as a dessert with a dollop of whipped cream atop.

SERVES 4.

Chilled Fresh Blackberry Soup

4 cups blackberries
4 teaspoons fresh lemon juice
6 tablespoons sugar
2 teaspoons potato flour
1/8 teaspoon salt
3/4 cup water
  Fresh lemon slices

Wash the blackberries and put them through a sieve. Stir in the lemon juice and set aside. Combine the sugar, potato flour, and salt in a saucepan. Blend in the water. Bring to a boil and stir in the blackberry juice mixture. Chill until slightly thickened and ready to serve. Serve in chilled cups. Garnish with slices of fresh lemon.

SERVES 4.

Norwegian Fruit Soup

    3 cups mixed raspberries, blueberries,
        and gooseberries
  4½ cups water
    3 tablespoons sugar
    5 thin slices lemon
    1 ounce blackberry brandy
    2 tablespoons potato flour
      Cold water
      Whipped cream

Clean the berries, rinse, and put in a pot with water, sugar, lemon slices, and blackberry brandy. Simmer until fruit is soft. Blend the potato flour with a little cold water and add to the berries. Stir well. Bring to a boil and then turn off heat. Serve in soup plates with a slice of cooked lemon in each dish. Serve hot or cold. If served cold, add a tablespoon of whipped cream to each portion.

SERVES 4.

The annual per capita consumption of potatoes in the United States is over 120 pounds, which averages out to one potato per person per day. In Germany, the per capita yearly consumption is about 375 pounds.

Golden Cheese Fondue

1 pound cheddar cheese, shredded
1½ tablespoons potato flour
1½ ounces bourbon
7 ounces club soda
1 teaspoon Worcestershire sauce
Dash Tabasco sauce
¼ teaspoon dry mustard
1 tablespoon butter
1 egg, lightly beaten
French or Italian bread, cut into chunks,
each with crust

In a bowl, toss the shredded cheese with the flour. Combine the bourbon, club soda, seasonings, and butter in a fondue pot or saucepan and bring to a simmer. Add the cheese a handful at a time, stirring constantly and allowing it to melt before adding more. Cook, stirring, until all cheese has melted and the mixture has thickened. Add a little of the hot cheese mixture to the beaten egg and then stir back into the pan. Stir smooth. Serve with chunks of bread for dipping.

SERVES 4.

Potatoes were once used for barter in America. In the November 28, 1858, *Democrat*, a newspaper published in Marshall, Missouri, there appeared a notice appealing to farmers who had not paid up their subscriptions. The publisher noted that he had to eat like everyone else and suggested that delinquents "who have cabbage, potatoes or anything of that kind can pay their indebtedness that way."

Deviled Lobster Tails

2 packages (9 ounces each) rock lobster
    tails
¼ cup butter
3 ounces potato flour
1 cup milk
1 teaspoon horseradish
¼ teaspoon cayenne
    Dash Worcestershire sauce
1 tablespoon chopped parsley
1 teaspoon salt
⅛ teaspoon pepper
2 teaspoons lemon juice
2 tablespoons fine bread crumbs
4 ounces Cognac
    Lemon wedges
    Parsley

Boil the lobster according to the directions on the package. Drain. Cut away the undershell, using scissors, and discard. Remove the meat and dice, reserving the shells. Melt the butter, add the flour, and blend. Gradually add the milk, horseradish, cayenne, Worcestershire sauce, parsley, salt, and pepper and cook over a low heat, stirring steadily until thickened. Add the lemon juice and lobster and mix well. Fill the lobster shells with the creamed mixture. Sprinkle with bread crumbs and arrange in a shallow baking dish. Bake in a preheated 400°F oven 10 minutes. Remove from the oven, spoon the Cognac over the lobster, and serve garnished with lemon wedges and parsley.

SERVES 4 TO 6.

Lobster au Whiskey

8 tablespoons butter
1¾ pounds lobster meat, cut into chunks
3 cups heavy cream, scalded
3 tablespoons potato flour
  Salt, pepper, and cayenne to taste
6 ounces bourbon

Heat 2 tablespoons of the butter in a heavy shallow pan. Sauté the lobster meat lightly. Add the cream and let simmer about 5 minutes. Knead 3 tablespoons of the butter with the flour and add to the lobster, stirring steadily with a wooden spoon until the mixture thickens. Season with salt, pepper, and cayenne. Let simmer another 5 minutes. Remove from fire. Pour in the bourbon and the remaining butter. Mix well and serve over steamed rice.

SERVES 6.

Brandied Seafood Shells

2 tablespoons butter
3 tablespoons potato flour
½ teaspoon seasoned salt
¼ teaspoon paprika
¼ teaspoon monosodium glutamate
⅛ teaspoon pepper
  Dash Worcestershire sauce
⅔ cup milk
⅓ cup Cognac
1 can (6½ ounces) crab meat, drained,
    boned, and flaked
2 hard-cooked eggs, chopped
1 tablespoon chopped parsley
2 tablespoons chopped chives

In a saucepan, melt the butter, add the flour, sea-soned salt, paprika, monosodium glutamate, pepper, and Worcestershire sauce, and blend. Gradually add the milk and Cognac and cook over a low heat, stirring constantly until thickened. Add the crab meat, eggs, parsley, and chives. Spoon into small seafood shells (clam or scallop will do). Bake in a preheated 350°F oven 10 minutes.

SERVES ABOUT 12.

Crab Meat with Spirits

¼ cup butter
2 cups sliced mushrooms
½ cup chopped green pepper
¼ cup chopped pimiento
1 medium-sized tomato, peeled and
    sliced
1 tablespoon minced shallots
6 tablespoons potato flour
2 cups light cream
1 pound crab meat
  Salt and pepper to taste
1 tablespoon chopped chives
2 ounces Scotch
  Steamed rice or noodles

Melt the butter in a large skillet. Add the mushrooms and green pepper and cook over a moderate heat 5 minutes, stirring constantly. Add the pimiento, tomato, and shallots. Cook 1 minute. Blend in the flour. Add the cream, stirring rapidly. Add the crab meat, salt, and pepper and heat until it bubbles. Add the chives and Scotch.

SERVES 4 TO 6.
SERVE WITH STEAMED RICE OR NOODLES.

Creamed Crab Meat

    4 tablespoons butter
    2 cups fresh mushrooms, sliced
    4 tablespoons chopped pimiento
    ½ cup celery, finely chopped
    1 tomato, peeled and cut into thin wedges
    1 tablespoon minced onion
    3 tablespoons potato flour
    2 cups light cream
    2 packages (6 ounces each) frozen crab
        meat, thawed, drained, and flaked
    ½ teaspoon salt
    ¼ teaspoon black pepper
    ¼ teaspoon paprika
    3 teaspoons minced chives
    2 ounces Calvados (apple brandy)
        Steamed rice

Melt the butter in a large skillet. Add the mushrooms, pimiento, celery, tomato, and onion. Cook 3 minutes. Sprinkle with the flour. Slowly add the cream, stirring constantly. Add the crab meat, salt, pepper, and paprika. Heat, stirring gently, until it bubbles. Add the chives and Calvados and simmer 3 more minutes. Serve over steamed rice.

SERVES 6.

Potato Handicrafts

There is scarcely a child who does not love french fries or mashed potatoes, but most kids don't know that potatoes are fun to play with too. Here are two low-cost, engrossing pastimes that will keep children happy for hours.

Potato Printing. With a few potatoes, a sharp knife, tempera paint, a paint brush, and a few dishes to put the paint in, kids can print everything from pictures to greeting cards.

Cut some potatoes in half with the knife—be careful of your fingers. On the flat end of the potato, cut a simple shape. Cut different ones on other flat pieces.

Pour some paint of different colors into the dishes. Paint should be about as thick as heavy cream. Add water if you need to.

Paint the shape you cut out on the potato with a little paint. Now press the potato firmly on a piece of paper or cloth. Use different shapes for different colors, but don't combine colors on one potato. Put the shapes together to make a picture.

Try this with letters cut on the potato and make a greeting card.

Shrunken Potato Heads. Assemble all your materials before you begin. You will need one potato, a stick about twelve inches long, two straight pins, two tiny buttons or sequins, an egg noodle, a large embroidery needle, heavy-duty thread, some wool or yarn, a knife, scissors, and glue.

Bake the potato slowly at 200°F at least two hours. It must be dry before you begin work. Allow the potato to cool.

Push the stick through one end of the potato, but not all the way through to the other end.

Make the eyes by pushing the straight pins through the buttons or sequins into the potato. Cut a few slits in the potato to make the nose. Make a slit for the mouth. Break the egg noodle into a few jagged pieces and insert them in the slit to make fanglike teeth.

Thread the needle but don't knot the end. Push the needle through the potato under the chin and out the other side. Cut off the thread, leaving about two inches hanging. Now the head has whiskers.

Cut yarn into short pieces to make bangs and lots of long ones to make the rest of the hair. Using glue, attach to the crown of the head so it looks like real hair.

Put your shrunken head on the radiator or in a very warm spot and it will get hard as a rock.

Creole Chicken

        1 chicken broiler (4 pounds), cup up
        1 teaspoon salt
        ½ teaspoon pepper
          Dash cayenne
        ¼ cup butter
        1 pound fresh mushrooms, thinly sliced
        1 cup water
        ½ cup Cognac
        1 beef bouillon cube
        2 tablespoons tomato paste
    1½ tablespoons potato flour
        1 tablespoon butter
        ½ cup pimiento strips

Sprinkle the chicken with salt, pepper, and cayenne. Heat ¼ cup butter in a large skillet. Add the chicken and brown well. Remove from the skillet and set aside. Add the mushrooms to the skillet. Cook uncovered 3 minutes, stirring steadily. Stir in the water, Cognac, bouillon cube, and tomato paste. Add the chicken. Bring to a boil. Simmer about 45 minutes until the chicken is done. Remove the chicken to a heated serving dish. Blend together the flour and 1 tablespoon butter and add to the skillet. Cook until thickened and boiling, stirring steadily. Gently stir in the pimiento strips and cook 1 minute more. Pour over the chicken.

SERVES 4.

Chicken Cacciatore

1 chicken fryer (3 pounds)
½ cup vegetable oil
1 clove garlic
2 teaspoons salt
½ teaspoon pepper
6 tablespoons potato flour
1 green pepper, sliced
1 medium-sized onion, sliced
1 can (16 ounces) tomatoes
¼ teaspoon celery seed
½ teaspoon ginger
2 tablespoons chopped parsley
2 tablespoons butter
½ pound mushrooms, sliced
¼ cup Sauternes wine

Cut the chicken into serving pieces. Heat the oil in a skillet, brown the garlic clove, and then remove it from the skillet. Rub the chicken pieces with salt, pepper, and flour. Brown the chicken. Add the green pepper and onion and sauté lightly. Add the tomatoes, celery seed, ginger, and parsley and simmer over a low heat for 30 minutes, until the chicken is tender. Melt the butter in a small skillet and sauté the mushrooms. Add the mushrooms and wine to the chicken. Cook over a high heat 5 minutes.

SERVES 4 TO 6.

Cranberry Chicken

¼ cup cooking oil
1 chicken broiler, cut into serving pieces
2 cups cranberry juice
1 tablespoon potato flour
1 tablespoon soy sauce
1 tablespoon vinegar
1 tablespoon sugar
¼ cup blanched almonds
¾ cup raisins
¾ cup quick-cooking rice
¼ teaspoon salt
1 green pepper, sliced in rounds
1 medium-sized onion, sliced in rings

Preheat the cooking oil in a frying pan to 250°F. Place the chicken in the pan and raise the temperature to 350°F. Cook, uncovered, 10 minutes, turning so that the chicken becomes golden brown on all sides. Pour the oil into a container for reuse. Add 1 cup of the cranberry juice mixed with the potato flour, soy sauce, vinegar, and sugar to the chicken in the frying pan. Cook, stirring, until the mixture is slightly thickened. Then turn the heat down to 250°F, cover, and simmer 15 minutes. Add the remaining cranberry juice, almonds, raisins, rice, salt, green pepper, and onion to the frying pan. Raise the temperature to bring to a boil and then turn down to 250°F and cook 10 more minutes with the lid on. Turn off the heat and let the chicken stand 5 minutes before serving.

SERVES 4.

Chicken Oriental-Style

1 cup bamboo shoots
2 cups diced celery
1 cup sliced onions
1 clove garlic, crushed
8 water chestnuts
6 ounces cooking oil
½ pound walnuts
1 pound chicken breasts, boned and cut
    into small pieces
¾ teaspoon salt
2 tablespoons potato flour
4 tablespoons soy sauce
1 teaspoon sugar
1 cup chicken broth

In a skillet, sauté the first 5 ingredients lightly in 1 ounce of the oil. Remove from the pan. Brown the walnuts in 4 ounces of the oil, remove, and drain. Dredge the chicken in a mixture of the salt, flour, soy sauce, and sugar. Sauté the chicken in the remaining 1 ounce of oil until tender. Add the chicken broth and heat thoroughly. Add the vegetables and nuts, heat, and serve.

SERVES 4.

Rhubarb Compote

¾ cup sugar
2 cups water
1½ pounds rhubarb, washed, scraped, and
      diced
½ teaspoon vanilla
3 tablespoons potato flour
¼ cup cold water

WHIPPED CREAM

1 cup chilled, heavy cream
¼ cup sugar
1 teaspoon vanilla
Dash cinnamon

Dissolve the sugar in water in a 2-quart saucepan and bring to a boil. Drop in the rhubarb, reduce the heat, and simmer, uncovered, 30 minutes, until the rhubarb shows no resistance when pierced with the tip of a sharp knife. Remove the pan from heat and stir in the vanilla. In a small bowl, mix the potato flour with the cold water to the consistency of a smooth paste. Gradually stir into the stewed rhubarb and bring to a boil, stirring steadily. Simmer 3 to 5 minutes, until mixture has thickened. Pour into a serving bowl and chill.

Make the Whipped Cream about 1 hour before you plan to serve the dessert. Combine all Whipped Cream ingredients in a bowl and beat until peaks form. Cover rhubarb with the Whipped Cream.

SERVES 6.

Passover Sponge Cake

    9 eggs, separated
 1½ cups sugar
  ½ cup cornstarch
  ¼ teaspoon salt
  ½ cup potato flour
  ⅛ teaspoon nutmeg
    1 tablespoon orange juice
    1 teaspoon orange rind

Beat the egg whites until stiff and gradually add ¾ cup of the sugar. Beat the egg yolks in a separate bowl with the remaining sugar. Sift the dry ingredients and beat into the egg yolks. Add the orange juice. Fold in the egg whites and orange rind. Bake in an ungreased tube pan in a preheated 325°F oven for 1 hour.

Scandinavian Cookies

    1 cup butter
    1 cup sugar
    1 cup heavy cream, whipped
    1 cup potato flour
    2 cups sifted all-purpose flour
 1½ cups chopped walnuts
  ¼ teaspoon nutmeg
    1 teaspoon vanilla

Cream the butter until light and fluffy. Beat in the sugar until the mixture whitens. Beat in the whipped cream. Stir in the potato flour, all-purpose flour, walnuts, nutmeg, and vanilla. Drop by teaspoonfuls onto greased cookie sheets. Bake in a preheated 350°F oven 10 to 12 minutes or until golden brown.

MAKES 50 TO 60 COOKIES.

Scandinavian Sponge Cake

2 tablespoons soft butter
2 tablespoons flour
4 eggs, separated
¼ cup sugar
½ teaspoon vanilla
    Dash nutmeg
¼ cup potato flour
¼ cup sifted, all-purpose flour

PASTRY CREAM

1 package unflavored gelatin
¼ cup cold water
¼ cup flour
2 cups light cream
¼ teaspoon salt
¾ cup sugar
8 egg yolks
2 teaspoons vanilla
¾ cup almonds, blanched and sliced

Spread an 11- by 16-inch jelly-roll pan with 1 table-spoon of the soft butter and line the pan with a 22-inch strip of wax paper, letting the paper extend over the narrower ends of pan. Spread the wax paper with the remaining butter, sprinkle it with 2 tablespoons flour, and tip from side to side to make sure the surface is covered evenly. Knock out any excess flour.

In a large mixing bowl, beat the egg whites with a balloon whisk until they form soft peaks. Beat in the sugar, 1 tablespoon at a time, and continue to beat vigorously until the egg whites form stiff peaks. Place the egg yolks in another large mixing bowl and stir gently for minute or so. Then stir in the vanilla and nutmeg. With a rubber spatula, mix a heaping teaspoon of the beaten egg whites into the yolks and then pour the mixture over the remaining egg whites in a bowl and sprinkle with the potato flour and regular flour. Fold all the ingredients together gently, using an under-cover, rather than a rotary, motion. When the egg whites are no longer visible, pour the mixture into the prepared jelly-roll pan and spread out evenly with a rubber spatula. Bake in a preheated 350°F oven 10 to 12 minutes, until the cake is a golden brown. Remove the pan from the oven and loosen the sides of the cake with a metal spatula or knife. Using the ends of the wax paper as handles, lift the cake out of the pan. Turn it over onto wax paper to cool and carefully peel off the original wax paper.

While the cake is cooling, prepare the Pastry Cream. Soften the gelatin 3 minutes in the cold water. In a 2-quart saucepan, beat the flour and ½ cup of the light cream with a wire whisk into a smooth paste. Then gradually beat in the rest of the cream, salt, and sugar. Cook over a moderate heat 1 or 2 minutes, still beating, until the mixture is thick and smooth. Remove from heat.

In a small bowl, combine ¼ cup of the hot sauce with the egg yolks. Slowly pour the mixture into the pan, whisking constantly. Cook over a low heat 1 to 2 minutes, stirring all the time, but do not let boil. Remove from heat and stir in the vanilla and softened gelatin. Set the Pastry Cream aside to cool.

When the cake has cooled to room temperature, slice it crosswise into 3 equal parts. Place 1 layer on a flat serving platter and spread ¼ of the cooled Pastry Cream over it. Place the second layer of cake on top, and spread another ¼ of Pastry Cream over it. Top with the third portion of cake and spread the top and sides with the remaining Pastry Cream. Gently press the almonds into the Pastry Cream all around and on top of the cake. Chill at least 2 hours before serving.

SERVES 4 TO 6.

8

THE POTATO AS
THE MAIN EVENT

Less than a century ago, the potato unadorned used to be the centerpiece at dinner in the humbler homes in Ireland, England, and much of Europe as well as parts of the United States. Boiled, baked, and fried, the tuber was the mainstay of the laboring man's diet, seasoned with salt and pepper and perhaps a little catsup. Then housewives began dressing up the spud with milk, butter, or cheese or a combination thereof and with a sprinkling of herbs to liven up the flavor. This was the precursor of today's hearty potato casseroles.

In England, the potato began to be used in dishes that included meat, fowl, or fish, giving birth to great stews, ragouts, and fricassees. They eventually found their way into haute cuisine when cooks began using wine and brandy to season them. Actually, the imaginative French were the ones who performed the greatest magic with the once simple meat and potato stews and fricassees. They were also responsible for other potato entrées such as Potato Cutlets, consisting of puréed potatoes baked gently with chicken livers, minced bacon, and sherry.

One main dish that gained favor in America, especially at luncheon, was the baked potato stuffed with everything from spinach and Mornay sauce to chipped beef.

Today few people are content with a plate of boiled potatoes and salt alone as were the Irish in olden times. But the spud, in one form or another, is still the main attraction on many a table.

Stuffed Potato with Chicken Livers

    4 medium-sized potatoes (about 1½
        pounds)
    ½ pound chicken livers, cut up
    ½ cup dairy sour cream
    3 tablespoons instant minced onion
    1 can (4 ounces) mushrooms, drained
      Paprika to taste

Pick potatoes of uniform size. Scrub and set directly on the oven rack. For nice crisp skins, do not rub with oil or wrap in foil. Bake in a preheated 400°F oven until tender, about 1 hour. Broil the chicken livers. Combine the sour cream and onion. Cut a lengthwise slice off the top of each potato. Remove the contents and rice or mash well. Then fold in the sour cream mixture. Add the broiled livers and mushrooms. Spoon the filling lightly into the potato shells. Sprinkle with paprika. Bake in a preheated 400°F oven until heated through and lightly browned.

SERVES 4.

In eighteenth-century Britain, the aristocracy accepted its privileged status as a natural right. Thus, when two Irish hairdressers decided to settle a spat on the field of honor, their seconds secretly loaded the pistols with boiled potatoes, on the grounds that a duel with real bullets was a matter only for gentlemen.

Potato Cutlets

2 pounds potatoes, peeled, cooked, and
    quartered
½ cup butter
½ teaspoon salt
⅛ teaspoon Tabasco sauce
¼ teaspoon paprika
1 egg yolk

CUTLET MIX

½ cup butter
10 chicken livers, finely chopped
¼ cup dry sherry
½ cup fresh mushrooms, sliced
¼ cup bacon, cooked well and crumbled
¼ teaspoon salt
¼ teaspoon cayenne
1 egg, beaten
1 cup dry bread crumbs

Drain the potatoes and let them dry. Mash, adding the butter, salt, Tabasco sauce, and paprika, and mix well over a low heat, stirring until smooth. Remove from heat, add the egg yolk, and mix about 5 minutes in the top of a double boiler to retain heat. Then make the Cutlet Mix.

Melt the butter in a pan and cook the chicken livers over a low heat until they are half done. Add the sherry, mushrooms, bacon, salt, and cayenne. Cook gently until the liquid is nearly absorbed. Form the mashed potatoes into patties, enclosing 1 heaping tablespoon of the liver mixture inside each. Dip them into the beaten egg and then into the bread crumbs. Place the cutlets in a buttered baking dish. Bake in a preheated 350°F oven about 15 minutes or until golden brown.

SERVES 4 TO 6.

Potatoes Stuffed with Chipped Beef

6 large potatoes, baked
½ pound dried beef, shredded
12 tablespoons butter
¼ cup all-purpose flour
2 cups milk, scalded
2 ounces Cognac
¼ teaspoon cayenne
  Paprika to taste

Cut a thick slice from the top of each potato, scoop out the pulp, and reserve the shells. Purée the pulp. In a skillet, sauté the dried beef in 6 tablespoons of the butter 5 minutes. Add the flour and cook the roux, stirring, 2 minutes. Add the scalded milk and Cognac and cook the mixture 5 minutes, stirring. Combine the potato purée with the chipped beef mixture and add the cayenne. Mound the mixture into reserved potato shells and put them in a preheated 350°F oven. Bake 10 to 15 minutes, until heated through. Top each potato with 1 tablespoon of the remaining butter. Sprinkle with paprika.

SERVES 6.

A few years ago, a British scholar came upon what is believed to be the first printed recipe for cooking potatoes. Published in Germany in 1851, it appeared in Max Rumpolt's *New Cookbook*. Here's the recipe: "Peel the potatoes. Cut in very small pieces. Boil in water, drain and dry in cloth. Roast in small pieces of bacon, add a little milk and simmer—then it will be good and tasty."

Potatoes Stuffed with Spinach

6 large potatoes, baked and halved
6 tablespoons butter
1¼ cups Mornay sauce
1 cup chopped, cooked spinach
  Salt, pepper, and paprika to taste
¼ teaspoon mace
  Grated Gruyère cheese
3 tablespoons butter, in bits
½ cup dried bread crumbs

MORNAY SAUCE

2 tablespoons flour
2 tablespoons butter, melted
1 cup milk, scalded
  Pinch salt
  Dash white pepper
  Dash nutmeg
2 egg yolks
1 heaping tablespoon grated Parmesan
  cheese
1 heaping tablespoon grated Swiss
  cheese

To make the Mornay Sauce, mix the flour and melted butter in a saucepan. Add the milk and stir well. Add the salt, pepper, and nutmeg. Let boil a few minutes on a low heat. Remove from the heat and mix in the egg yolks and grated cheeses. Stir until the cheese melts.

Scoop out the pulp from the potatoes and reserve the shells. Purée the potato pulp and add 6 tablespoons butter, the Mornay sauce, spinach, salt, pepper, paprika, and mace. Combine the mixture well and mound into the potato shells. Sprinkle with the Gruyère cheese, butter bits, and bread crumbs. Put the stuffed potatoes under the broiler until browned.

SERVES 6.

Stuffed Potatoes Provençale

    6 large potatoes, baked and halved
    2 hard-cooked egg yolks, sieved
    1 cup green pepper, finely diced
    ¼ cup thick tomato purée
    ¼ cup canned tuna fish packed in oil
        Salt and pepper to taste
    ⅛ teaspoon Tabasco sauce
    ⅓ cup dried bread crumbs
    2 ounces olive oil
        Fines Herbes (mixture of parsley,
            chervil, chives, and tarragon)

Scoop out the pulp from the potato shells and reserve the shells. Purée the pulp, adding the sieved egg yolks, green pepper, tomato purée, tuna fish, salt, pepper, and Tabasco sauce. Fill the potato shells with the mixture and sprinkle with the bread crumbs and olive oil. Heat the stuffed potatoes in a 375° oven about 15 minutes. Sprinkle with Fines Herbes and serve.

SERVES 6.

The baked potato is becoming so popular out West that it is competing with the hot dog and hamburger trade.

A fast-food house named One Potato Two is doing a flourishing business, offering baked spuds in Minneapolis, Minnesota, and Madison, Wisconsin. Customers can have their choice of twenty-eight stuffings, including bacon bits, chili, crab meat, and yogurt. The house slogan is "meal in a peel."

In Seattle, Washington, a restaurant named The Price Is Right offers a regular dinner, except that the entrée is not meat but a baked potato. It is offered topped with poached eggs and hollandaise sauce or accompanied by a host of side dishes, including creamed spinach, chopped tomatoes sautéed in butter, and Swiss cheese. The motto of this house is "honor thy potato."

Potatoes Stuffed with Bacon

6 large potatoes, baked
1 cup chopped shallots
3 tablespoons butter
½ cup well-cooked bacon, crumbled
1 cup diced green pepper
1 tablespoon chili powder
Salt and cayenne to taste
Chopped chives

Cut a thick slice from the top of each potato, scoop out the pulp, and reserve the deep shells. In a skillet, sauté the shallots in 1 tablespoon of the butter until soft. Purée the potato pulp, adding the bacon bits, green pepper, and sautéed shallots. Add the chili powder, salt, and cayenne and mix well. Heap the mixture into the potato shells. Melt the remaining butter and sprinkle over the potato shells. Put them in a preheated 375°F oven 10 to 15 minutes, until heated through. Sprinkle with chopped chives and serve.

SERVES 6.

Pommes de Terre Langouste

8 medium-sized potatoes, baked
1 cup soft butter
Salt and pepper
1 pound cooked shrimp
1 can (10½ ounces) frozen condensed
    cream of shrimp soup
1 cup dairy sour cream
2 tablespoons tomato paste
1 teaspoon dill weed
1 cup cherry tomatoes

Cut the potatoes in half and scoop out the pulp, discarding the shells. Mash roughly with a fork, working in ½ cup of the butter and the salt and pepper. Rub the rest of the butter into a 6-cup mold. Press about half of the shrimp on the top and sides of the mold. Press the potatoes carefully into the mold, pushing down firmly after each addition. Heat the soup until it is hot. Add the sour cream, tomato paste, and dill. Heat the mold in a preheated 350°F oven to loosen the potatoes. Unmold and heat in the oven if necessary. Spoon the hot sauce over the potatoes and garnish with tomatoes and the rest of the shrimp.

SERVES 8.

American author Mark Twain was a meat-and-potato man, a son of the frontier who never lost his love of American food despite years of epicurean fare consumed during his lecture tours in Europe. In fact, when he and his family were living in London, he brought over his American housekeeper of many years, partly because he had decided that no English cook could make creamed potatoes the way she did.

One of Mark Twain's fondest memories was of when he was a fifteen-year-old apprentice on a weekly newspaper in Hannibal, Missouri. He and a colleague used to steal potatoes from the editor's cellar and cook them on the print shop's stove. Years later, when he had become a famous figure, Mark Twain was the guest of honor at a lavish banquet hosted by Kaiser Wilhelm II of Germany. The one thing the writer remembered about the royal menu was the kind of potato served. It seems that it reminded him of the midnight feasts he used to consume in the Hannibal print shop.

Potato Snow for Chicken Stew

1 stewing chicken (4 to 5 pounds), cut up
Water
1 yellow onion stuck with 3 cloves
Parsley sprigs
Celery leaves
1 bay leaf
4 medium-sized potatoes, peeled and
halved
3 tablespoons butter
3 tablespoons flour
Salt and pepper to taste
1 tablespoon lemon juice
1 egg yolk
1 package (10 ounces) frozen peas
¼ cup melted butter
Paprika

Put the chicken in a large pot and cover with water. Add the onion, parsley, celery, and bay leaf. Bring to a boil and then reduce the heat. Simmer until the chicken is tender, 1 hour or longer. Strain the broth and set aside 2 cups. Half an hour before serving, boil the potatoes. Melt the butter, blend in the flour, and gradually add the broth that was set aside. When the mixture is smooth, add the salt, pepper, and lemon juice. Add the egg yolk and peas. Remove the skin from the chicken and keep the chicken warm in a serving dish. Pour the sauce over the chicken and top with snow by forcing hot, boiled potatoes through a ricer or sieve. Let the potatoes fall lightly; do not pack. Sprinkle with melted butter and paprika.

SERVES 4.

Springtime Beef Stew

Salad oil
3 pounds stew beef, cut into 2-inch cubes
Salt and pepper to taste
1 can (10½ ounces) condensed beef broth
½ cup brandy
Peel of 1 orange, coarsely grated
6 medium-sized potatoes, peeled and quartered
2 large celery stalks, sliced
2 tablespoons butter
2 large celery stalks, sliced
¼ cup walnuts, coarsely chopped
3 or 4 soda crackers, crumbled

Heat the oil in a Dutch oven. Brown the meat on all sides. Season with salt and pepper. Add the broth, brandy, and orange peel. Cover and cook over a medium-low heat 2 hours. Add the potatoes and cook 30 minutes more or until tender. Meanwhile, sauté the celery in butter 5 minutes. Add the walnuts to the celery and set aside. When the meat and potatoes are done, arrange them in a serving bowl and keep warm. Pour the stew juices and orange peel in an electric blender along with the cracker crumbs. Blend on a low speed until smooth. Return the mixture to the pan and bring to a boil, stirring. Pour the hot sauce over the meat and potatoes. Garnish with celery and walnuts.

SERVES 6.

Shepherd Pie

1 medium-sized onion, chopped
1 cup chopped celery
3 tablespoons butter
3 cups cooked roast beef, coarsely ground
    or diced
1 teaspoon oregano
    Salt and pepper to taste
4 cups seasoned mashed potatoes
2 tablespoons grated Parmesan cheese
    Paprika

In a skillet, sauté the onion and celery in the butter until tender. Stir in the meat and oregano. Season to taste and heat through. Pour the mixture into a buttered shallow 2-quart casserole. Spoon the mashed potatoes over the hash. Sprinkle with cheese and paprika. Bake in a preheated 350°F oven 40 minutes.

SERVES 6.

Meatball Potato Pie

3 cups water
4 tablespoons butter
1 teaspoon salt
1 cup milk
4 cups instant mashed potato flakes
1½ pound ground chuck
1 small onion, finely chopped
1 egg, beaten
1 can (8 ounces) tomato sauce
    Salt and pepper to taste
¼ teaspoon basil
½ teaspoon sugar
1 package (8 ounces) mozzarella cheese,
    sliced
1 tablespoon melted butter

Combine the water, butter, and salt in a saucepan. Bring to a boil. Remove from heat and stir in the milk and instant potato flakes. Set aside to cool. Combine the meat, onion, egg, and ¼ cup of the tomato sauce. Season with salt and pepper. Butter a 10-inch oven-proof skillet and gently press the mashed potatoes against the sides to form a crust. Shape the meat into 8 to 10 meatballs and place in the potato crust. Mix the rest of the tomato sauce with the basil and sugar. Pour over the meatballs. Top with cheese. Brush the potato crust with the melted butter. Bake in a preheated 400°F oven 40 minutes, until the potatoes are golden

SERVES 6.

Italian Stuffed Baked Potatoes
by Louis Evans

Louis Evans is executive chef at the famed Pontchartrain in New Orleans, a city widely known for its epicurean centers.

6 medium-sized Idaho baking potatoes
 Salt and pepper to taste
¼ cup milk
¼ cup heavy cream
2 tablespoons butter, melted
1 cup grated Parmesan cheese

Wash and dry the potatoes. Bake them in a preheated 400°F oven until they are soft. Cut off a lengthwise slice from each potato. Scoop out the pulp, leaving the shells intact. Place the potato shells in the oven to become dry and crisp. Mash the pulp and add the salt, pepper, and enough of the milk and cream to give a fluffy consistency. Put the mixture into a pastry bag and pipe into the shells, rounding them over the tops. Brush with melted butter and sprinkle with Parmesan cheese. Bake in a preheated 400°F oven until browned.

SERVES 6.

Pennsylvania Dutch Potatoes and Franks

6 medium-sized potatoes (about 2
    pounds), cooked, peeled, and diced
2 green onions, chopped
6 dinner-size frankfurters, sliced ½-inch
    thick
2 tablespoons bacon drippings or salad
    oil
2 tablespoons sugar
1 teaspoon flour
1 teaspoon salt
¼ cup vinegar
½ cup water
1 tablespoon chopped parsley

In a large serving bowl, combine the hot potatoes with the green onions. Cover and keep warm. Meanwhile, in a large skillet over a medium heat, brown the frankfurters in the bacon drippings or salad oil. With a slotted spoon, remove the frankfurters, reserving the fat. Add the frankfurters to the potatoes and onions and keep warm. Into the hot drippings, stir the sugar, flour, and salt until smooth and bubbly. Gradually stir in the vinegar and water. Cook, stirring constantly, until the sauce thickens and boils. Pour the sauce over the potatoes and frankfurters. Sprinkle with parsley.

SERVES 6.

Fruited Pork Chops with Potatoes

6 pork chops, about 1 inch thick
  Salt and pepper to taste
1 package (12 ounces) mixed dried fruits
  Peel of one orange, cut in a spiral
1 cup water
6 medium-sized potatoes (about 2
    pounds), peeled and quartered
3 ginger snaps
  Water

In a heavy skillet or Dutch oven, brown the chops and season. Arrange 3 chops in the same pan. Add the dried fruit, first removing the pits from the prunes. Cover the fruit with the other 3 chops. Add the orange peel and water. Cover and simmer over a low heat 15 minutes. Add the potatoes, cover, and cook slowly 45 minutes more, until the potatoes are tender. To serve, arrange the chops, fruit, and potatoes on a warm serving platter. Moisten the ginger snaps with a little water and crumble into the pan juices. Cook, stirring constantly, until the sauce is smooth. Add more water, if necessary. Pour the sauce, removing the orange peel, over the meat or serve separately.

SERVES 6.

Chicken Fricassee Potato Dumplings

    1 chicken broiler-fryer (about 4 pounds),
        cut up
    7 medium-sized potatoes (about 2½
        pounds), peeled
    1 medium-sized onion, sliced
    2 stalks celery, chopped
    2 cloves garlic, crushed
    4 teaspoons salt
    ¼ teaspoon pepper
    6 cups water
    1 package (10 ounces) frozen peas and
        carrots
    ½ cup flour
    1 cup water

POTATO DUMPLINGS
    1 potato, cooked in broth
    1 egg, lightly beaten
    ¼ cup flour
    1 tablespoon chopped parsley
    Salt and pepper to taste

In a large kettle, combine the chicken, potatoes, onion, celery, garlic, salt, pepper, and water. Bring to a boil. Reduce the heat, cover, and simmer 45 minutes or until the chicken is tender. If desired, the meat can be separated from the skin and bones and then cut up and returned to the sauce. Add the frozen vegetables and cook 10 minutes. To make the Potato Dumplings, remove 1 potato from the broth. Mash with a fork to measure 1 cup potato. Mix lightly with the remaining dumpling ingredients. Thicken the broth with the ½ cup of flour, mixed to a thin paste with the water. Cook 3 minutes. Then drop the dumpling mixture, by tablespoons, into the simmer-ing sauce. When the dumplings rise to the surface, cover the pan and simmer 12 to 15 minutes. To serve, place 2 dumplings into each soup plate. Ladle the meat and sauce over them.

SERVES 6.

It is said that the potato came into its own through the poor people of Northern Europe. But nowhere was poverty so bitter and the potato so welcome as in Ireland. The Irish lavished pet names on the tuber. Priests and altar boys blessed the fields with holy water. The average adult in the Emerald Isle was said to eat from eight to ten pounds of potatoes in a single day. The potato blight of 1847, which decimated Ireland's population, taught the Irish not to place too much trust in the spud, but they are still con-vinced that a day without potatoes is a day without sufficient nourishment. Boiled in its jacket and served plain, mashed with chopped scallions and rich dairy cream, or cooked in any of a score of other ways, the potato is served at the table at least once each day.

Visitors to Ireland in 1945 after the austerity diet of war-ravaged Europe (Ireland had remained neutral in the conflict), were enthralled by such dishes as potato cakes dripping in butter and boxty, the traditional dish eaten on Shrove Tuesday. Boxty is composed of both grated raw and mashed cooked potatoes with a binding of flour. It can be baked on a griddle or pan-fried, but Irish cooks always remember one thing—to stir into the mixture a ring wrap-ped in paper, which foretells an early marriage for the lucky finder.

Ireland's fondness for the potato comes through in the terms it uses. The Irish, to my knowledge, never refer to a "potato field" but call it "the potato garden." Even the names given the tuber are colorful: Ulster Chieftain, Aran Banner, and Skerry Champion.

Pastel de Choclo—A Leftover Feast

2 medium-sized onions, chopped
1 clove garlic, minced
1 tablespoon salad oil
2 cups cooked roast beef, diced
1 cup beef broth
¼ cup raisins
¼ cup stuffed olives
1 teaspoon salt
1 teaspoon cumin seed
1 teaspoon oregano
⅛ teaspoon pepper
2 cups potatoes, peeled, cooked, and
   cubed
6 hard-cooked eggs, sliced

CRUST

2 tablespoons steak sauce
½ package (11 ounces) piecrust mix

In a skillet, sauté the onions and garlic in the oil. Add the beef, broth, raisins, olives, and seasonings. Simmer, uncovered, ½ hour or until the liquid is reduced by half. Add the potatoes and pour into a 2-quart baking dish. Arrange the egg slices on top.

To make the Crust, blend the steak sauce with the piecrust mix, omitting the water. Roll out to fit the top of the baking dish. Transfer the crust to the baking dish, pinching the edges to seal. Decorate with pastry scraps. Bake in a preheated 375°F oven 35 to 40 minutes or until the crust is golden. Serve hot.

SERVES 6 TO 8.

Butter Birds and Baked Potatoes

1 cup soft butter
1 clove garlic, crushed
1 tablespoon chopped chives
2 tablespoons chopped parsley
1 teaspoon salt
6 whole chicken breasts, boned
¼ cup milk
1 package (2⅜ ounces) seasoned coating
    mix
6 large baking potatoes
1 cup heavy cream
1 cup dairy sour cream
1 cup cottage cheese
  Salt and pepper to taste
  Canned sliced beets

Mix the butter, garlic, chives, parsley, and salt. Pat into a long roll on waxed paper. Roll up and chill firm. Pound the chicken breasts flat, keeping the skins intact. Divide the rolled butter into 6 chunks and roll the chicken tightly around the butter, securing firmly with picks. Dip each piece in the milk and coat heavily with the seasoned coating mix. Arrange in a shallow baking pan. Set the oven at 400°F. The potatoes go in 15 minutes ahead of the chicken. Do not wrap the potatoes in foil. Bake the potatoes 60 minutes, and the chicken 45 minutes. Whirl the heavy cream, sour cream, and cottage cheese in a blender. Season with salt and pepper. Knead and split the potatoes and scoop the flesh onto a hot platter, discarding the skins. Arrange the chicken on top with sauce, and garnish with sliced beets.

SERVES 6.

Greek Stefado for a Feast

2 pounds small potatoes, fresh or frozen
2 cups canned tomatoes
1 can (6 ounces) tomato paste
¾ cup red wine
2 tablespoons vinegar
2 teaspoons salt
4 pounds veal or lamb shanks, sliced
    through bone
¼ cup olive oil
1 pound small boiling onions
3 bay leaves
    Lemon peel, 3-inch strip
½ cup blanched almonds or pecans
¼ pound Greek feta or other light cheese
    such as Monterey Jack

Peel the potatoes and slice in half lengthwise. Blend the tomatoes, tomato paste, wine, vinegar, and salt in a blender. In a saucepan, brown the meat on all sides in the oil. Set the meat aside and brown the potatoes and onions. Return the meat to the pot with the vegetables, tomato mixture, bay leaves, and lemon peel. Cover tightly and simmer 1½ hours, until the meat is tender. Add the nuts and crumble cheese over the sauce. Continue cooking until the cheese melts slightly and blends with the sauce.

SERVES 6.

Baked Stuffed Potatoes

by Stig Felbig

Stig Felbig is executive chef at the Clift Hotel in San Francisco. He is a graduate of the Chef's School in Copenhagen, where he began his career.

2 cups rock salt
12 Idaho baking potatoes, about 8 ounces each
1½ cups milk
¼ pound butter
   Seasoned salt to taste
8 ounces cream cheese
¼ cup green onions, finely sliced
¼ cup chives, chopped
   Melted butter

Sprinkle enough of the rock salt in the bottom of a baking pan to make a ¼-inch layer. Arrange the potatoes on the salt without crowding. Bake in a preheated 350°F oven until the potatoes are done, about 1 hour. Cut off the top third of each potato and scoop out the pulp, reserving shells. Put the pulp through a food mill while still warm, to avoid any lumps. Warm the milk and melt the butter in it. Mix the potatoes with an electric mixer and add enough of the warmed milk and butter to give the consistency of creamy mashed potatoes. Add the seasoned salt, cream cheese, green onions, and chives. Fill the potato shells with the mixture. Drizzle a little melted butter atop each stuffed shell. Bake in a preheated 350°F oven about 30 minutes, until the potatoes are heated through.

SERVES 12.

Muscovite Pigeons

1½ cups dehydrated hashed brown
    potatoes
1 pound ground beef or lamb
1 small onion, minced
1 teaspoon dill weed
1 cup buttermilk
2 eggs
  Salt and pepper to taste
1 head cabbage
  Boiling water
1 cup beef bouillon
1 tablespoon brown sugar
  Dairy sour cream
  Tomato sauce

Mix the potatoes (uncooked), meat, onion, dill, buttermilk, and eggs. Season with salt and pepper. Blanch the cabbage in the boiling water to unfurl the leaves. Pat the leaves dry. Spoon the filling into the center of each leaf, tuck in the sides, and roll them up. Secure with toothpicks. Set the rolls in a large casserole. Mix the bouillon with the brown sugar and pour over all. Cover tightly and bake in a preheated 350°F oven 1½ hours. Serve with sour cream and tomato sauce or a mixture of the two.

SERVES 6.

Camper's Choucroute Garnie

    4 thick slices bacon
    1 can (1 pound 11 ounces) sauerkraut
    1 canned ham (1 pound), sliced
    1 can (8 ounces) Vienna sausages
    1 can (7½ ounces) tongue, sliced
    2 pounds small whole potatoes, boiled
        and peeled
 ¼ cup freeze-dried chives
    2 cloves garlic, crushed
      Beer
      Salt and pepper to taste

In a Dutch oven or heavy pan, fry the bacon until it is half crisp. Drain the sauerkraut and mix it with the bacon and drippings. Arrange the sliced meats and sausages on one side of the pot, the drained potatoes on the other. Sprinkle with chives and garlic. Pour in the beer to almost cover. Sprinkle lightly with salt and heavily with pepper. Cover tightly and simmer 30 minutes, until everything is hot.

SERVES 4.

Deep Dish Pot Pie

POTATO CRUST

 1 cup dehydrated hashed brown potatoes
 1 egg, beaten
 2 tablespoons melted butter
 1½ teaspoons baking powder
 ⅔ cup sifted flour

FILLING

 1 medium-sized onion, finely chopped
 2 tablespoons oil
 1 pound ground beef
 1 can (12 ounces) corn with red and
   green peppers, drained
 ½ teaspoon salt
 1½ teaspoons chili powder
   Freshly ground pepper to taste
 1 can (11 ounces) chili beef soup,
   undiluted
 1 egg, beaten

Rehydrate the hashed brown potatoes according to the directions on the package and drain thoroughly. Add the remaining ingredients for the Potato Crust and mix well. Form into a ball, cover, and refrigerate while the Filling is being made.

Cook the onion in the oil until soft. Add the ground beef and brown. Add the remaining Filling ingredients except the beaten egg and continue cooking until all the ingredients are blended. Spoon into a large casserole.

Roll out the Potato Crust to a ¼-inch thickness and fit over the casserole. Brush with a little beaten egg. Bake in a preheated 375°F oven 25 to 30 minutes or until the crust is lightly browned.

SERVES 4.

Tofelspitz

2 medium-sized carrots
1 medium-sized parsnip
½ small celery root, *optional*
3 pounds beef brisket
¼ pound cubed beef liver
1 celery heart including leaves
1 medium-sized onion, finely chopped
1 leek (white part only)
5 cups water
2 teaspoons salt
6 medium-sized potatoes, peeled and cut
    in half
  Paprika to taste
½ cup light cream
  Parsley sprigs

Peel and cut the carrots, parsnip, and celery root into 2-inch strips. Put in a large pot and add the brisket, liver, celery, onion, leek, water, and 1 teaspoon of the salt. Bring to a boil, reduce the heat, cover, and simmer 2½ hours. Add the potatoes. Simmer 30 minutes or until the meat is tender. Remove the brisket and potatoes. Strain the broth and set aside 2½ cups. Return the meat and potatoes to the pot, cover with remaining broth, and keep hot until ready to serve. Purée the vegetables, liver, and reserved broth in a blender. Pour into a pan and stir in the remaining 1 teaspoon of salt, paprika, and light cream. Simmer 5 minutes and serve with parsley sprigs. Remove the brisket and potatoes from the broth. Slice the meat and arrange on a platter surrounded by potatoes.

SERVES 6.

Balkan Potato Boats

6 large potatoes
  Butter
  Parmesan cheese, grated
1 pound ground beef
1 tablespoon anise seed
1 egg
1 clove garlic, crushed
1 small onion, minced
1 teaspoon salt
  Vegetable oil
  Green peppers
  Onions
  Mushrooms
  Melted butter

Cut a lengthwise wedge from each potato. Rub the cut edge with butter and sprinkle the surfaces with cheese. Put them on a cookie sheet and bake in a preheated 400°F oven about 40 minutes, until almost done. Meanwhile, mix the beef with the anise seed, egg, garlic, minced onion, and salt. Shape into small meatballs and brown lightly in a skillet in a little hot oil. String on metal skewers with small chunks of pepper and onion. Finish off with a mushroom half. Set the skewers on the potatoes and continue baking 15 minutes, basting with melted butter.

SERVES 6.

Braised Potatoes

¼ pound bacon, diced
2 pounds potatoes, peeled and cut into
      chunks
4 large tomatoes, peeled and quartered

2 cloves garlic, crushed
½ teaspoon thyme
1 cup pitted black olives
½ pound small mushrooms
Salt and pepper to taste
Cognac

Cook the bacon in a casserole until it is half done. Arrange the potatoes and tomatoes in the casserole and rub with garlic and thyme. Add the olives and mushrooms. Sprinkle with salt and pepper. Pour a small glass of Cognac over all. Cover and bake in a preheated 350°F oven 45 minutes, until the potatoes are done.

SERVES 4.

Danish Burning Love

3 pounds potatoes, peeled and cut into
    chunks
1 pound slab bacon, cut into ½-inch
    cubes
2 large onions, sliced
4 tablespoons butter
¾ cup milk
Salt to taste
1 can (4¼ ounces) cubed beets
⅓ cup chopped parsley

Cook the potatoes in boiling water until tender. Cook the bacon cubes in a frying pan until crisp. Add the onions and cook until golden brown. Drain the potatoes and mash coarsely with the butter, milk, and salt. Heap the potatoes onto a serving platter, top with the bacon and onions, sprinkle with cubed beets and parsley, and serve hot.

SERVES 4.

Scallop-Potato Casserole

    4 medium-sized potatoes, peeled and
        thinly sliced
    4 tablespoons melted butter
    2 tablespoons grated Parmesan cheese
    2 cups dry white wine
      Juice of ½ lemon
    2 green onion tops, chopped
    ¼ teaspoon thyme
    1 bay leaf
    2 sprigs parsley
    ¾ teaspoon salt
    ¼ teaspoon pepper
    ¼ teaspoon Tabasco sauce
    1 pound mushrooms, sliced
    3 pounds scallops
      Water
    ¼ pound butter
    ½ cup flour
    2 cups light cream
    2 egg yolks
    2 tablespoons minced parsley

Butter a cookie sheet. Arrange overlapping slices of potatoes on the cookie sheet into 2 circles. Drizzle melted butter over them. Sprinkle with cheese. Bake in a pre-heated 400° oven 30 minutes.

In a saucepan, bring the wine, lemon juice, green onion tops, spices, and seasonings to a boil. Simmer 5 minutes. Add the mushrooms, scallops, and enough water to barely cover them. Simmer gently 5 minutes. Remove the scallops, quarter them, and set aside. Remove the mushrooms. Discard the parsley sprigs and bay leaf. Boil the liquid to reduce it to 2 cups and reserve.

In another saucepan, melt the butter, stir in the flour, and allow to bubble a few minutes. Add the cream and reserved broth and cook over a medium heat, stirring constantly, until thickened. Remove from heat. Place the egg yolks in a bowl and beat with a fork. Pour a little of the hot sauce into the yolks and mix well. Add this mixture, gradually, to the sauce. Return the scallops and mushrooms to the sauce. Stir in the minced parsley. Pour the scallop mixture into 2 greased 2-quart casseroles. Slide a ring of baked potato slices onto the top of each casserole. Spoon a little of the sauce over the potatoes. Bake in a preheated 350°F oven 30 minutes.

SERVES 5.

Clam and Egg Hash

12 ounces dehydrated hashed brown
    potatoes
¼ cup butter
¼ cup oil
1 large onion, chopped
2 cans (7½ ounces each) minced clams,
    drained
   Salt and pepper to taste
4 egg yolks
6 tablespoons grated Parmesan cheese
¼ cup freeze-dried chives
6 tablespoons evaporated milk

Cook the potatoes according to the directions on the package. Drain well. Melt the butter with the oil in a heavy skillet and cook the onion. Mix the potatoes with the clams and season. Press them into the skillet with a spatula. Brown well, turning often. Mix the egg yolks with the cheese, chives, and evaporated milk. Pour gently over the hash. Cover and cook until the eggs are just set.

SERVES 4.

Familjens Raddning

 4 large potatoes, baked
 ½ cup buttermilk
 2 tablespoons butter
   Salt and pepper to taste
 1 teaspoon dill weed
 1 pound cooked shrimp
 4 hard-cooked eggs, sliced
 2 large tomatoes, cut in half
 1 can (1 pound) young peas
 1 can (1 pound) small whole beets
 ½ cup browned bread crumbs

Slit the skins of the baked potatoes and scoop out the flesh onto a warm platter, discarding the skins. Heat the buttermilk in a saucepan and melt the butter in it. Pour over the potatoes and sprinkle with salt, pepper, and dill. Arrange the shrimp, egg slices, tomatoes, peas, and beets decoratively on a platter. Sprinkle with bread crumbs. Slip under the broiler to heat thoroughly.

SERVES 4.

Lovely Lemon Potatoes

 2 pounds potatoes, peeled and cut into
     large chunks
   Boiling salted water
 1 large onion, coarsely chopped
   Grated rind and juice of 1 large lemon
 2 tablespoons flour
 4 tablespoons butter

¼ cup chopped parsley
¼ teaspoon nutmeg
   Salt and pepper to taste

Parboil the potatoes in the boiling salted water 4 minutes. Drain. Toss with all the ingredients except the lemon juice. Transfer to a casserole and bake in a pre-heated 450°F oven until the potatoes are tender. Just before serving, squeeze the lemon juice over all.

SERVES 6.

Swiss Potato Torte

5 medium-sized potatoes, peeled and
   coarsely grated
2 medium onions, grated
2½ cups Gruyère or Swiss cheese, grated
1 teaspoon salt
½ teaspoon pepper
¼ teaspoon nutmeg
   Butter
   Parsley
   Freshly cooked vegetables

Mix potatoes, onions, cheese, pepper, and nutmeg thoroughly. Butter an 8- by 3½-inch springform pan. Pour the potato mixture into the pan and bake in a pre-heated 450°F oven 1 hour, until golden brown. Turn the torte out onto a platter, garnish with parsley and freshly cooked vegetables.

SERVES 6.

Burnished Vegetables of Indochina

4 large potatoes
1 small head cauliflower
  Boiling water
1 pound mixed squash (zucchini,
    crookneck, and patty pan)
2 teaspoons turmeric
1 pint plain yogurt
1 teaspoon dry mustard
3 teaspoons grated ginger root or
    candied ginger
1 bunch of watercress leaves, chopped
  Salt and pepper to taste
  Diced green onions

Peel the potatoes. Slice two of the potatoes in half lengthwise and cut them into strips. Cut the remaining potatoes into decorative shapes. Cook the potatoes with the whole cauliflower in a steamer with boiling water 12 minutes. Add the squash. Sprinkle the vegetables with 1 teaspoon of the turmeric and continue cooking another 12 minutes, until all the vegetables are just tender. Cut up the cauliflower and squash. Mix the yogurt with the other teaspoon of turmeric, mustard, ginger, and watercress. Season with salt and pepper. Spoon the sauce over the steamed vegetables, sprinkle with green onions, and serve.

SERVES 6.

Chiles Rellenos

¼ cup butter
¼ cup milk
   Salt and pepper to taste
1½ cups grated cheddar cheese
  1 cup mashed potatoes
  2 cans (4 ounces each) green chilies
   Flour
   Fat for deep frying
  2 cans (8 ounces each) tomato sauce

Add the butter, milk, salt, pepper, and cheese to the mashed potatoes. Remove the seeds from the chilies. Fill the chilies with the potato mixture using a spoon or pastry tube. Dust with flour and fry in deep fat, turning once. Serve hot with the tomato sauce.

SERVES 4.

Potato and Beef Sandwich Casserole

1½ cups dry bread crumbs
2 cups tomato juice
2 eggs, lightly beaten
1 pound ground beef
1 teaspoon oregano
1 teaspoon salt
½ teaspoon pepper
4 large potatoes (6 to 8 ounces each), peeled
2 tomatoes, thickly sliced
2 medium-sized onions, thickly sliced
1 cup grated American cheese
Paprika

In a large bowl, moisten the bread crumbs with ½ cup of the tomato juice and the eggs. Add the meat, oregano, salt, and pepper and mix well. Cut the potatoes lengthwise into medium-thick slices. Shape ⅙ of the meat mixture into a pattie. Sandwich the pattie between two potato slices. Repeat to make six sandwiches. In a deep, rectangular 2-quart casserole, arrange the sandwiches in a row, standing on lengthwise edge. Tuck the tomato and onion slices between the sandwiches. Arrange extra potato slices around the edge of the casserole. Pour the remaining tomato juice over the casserole. Cover and bake in a preheated 400°F oven 1 hour or until the potatoes and meat are done. Sprinkle with cheese and paprika and return to the oven to melt the cheese. Serve each person a sandwich with some tomato, onion, and potato slices on the side.

SERVES 6.

Hutsepot

4½ pounds beef rump roast
3 quarts water
2 bay leaves
5 whole black peppercorns
1 tablespoon salt
1½ pounds Italian sausages
2 pounds potatoes, peeled and cut into
    chunks
1 medium-sized head savoy cabbage, cut
    in wedges
5 medium-sized carrots, cut into thirds
1 package (10 ounces) frozen peas,
    thawed
Croutons
Green onions, sliced
Mustard
Horseradish

Put the beef in a large, heavy pot and cover with water. Add the bay leaves, peppercorns, and salt. Simmer, covered, 2 hours. Add the sausages, potatoes, cabbage, and carrots. Continue simmering 30 minutes. Add the peas and cook 7 to 10 minutes. Garnish with croutons and green onions. Serve with mustard and horseradish on the side.

SERVES 8.

Shortcut Pot au Feu

3 pounds beef short ribs
1 large onion
3 cloves
  Water
6 medium-sized carrots, cut into halves
½ teaspoon thyme
1 bay leaf
2 pounds chicken legs and thighs
3 pounds potatoes, peeled and quartered
  Salt
  Horseradish
  Mustard
  French bread

Have the short ribs cut into 1½-inch slices. Put the beef, onion, and cloves into a heavy kettle and add water to cover. Cover and simmer 30 minutes. Add the carrots, thyme, bay leaf, chicken, potatoes, and salt and continue cooking 45 mintues. Strain the broth and serve separately in mugs. Serve the ribs, chicken, and vegetables in soup bowls accompanied by horseradish, mustard, and crusty French bread.

SERVES 6.

Halberstadt Meat and Drink in a Pot

1 pound salt pork
3 carrots, peeled and sliced
3 bay leaves
1 bunch parsley, chopped

12 dried figs
2 pounds onions, peeled and cut into
    wedges
1½ pounds lean stew beef
1 pound lean pork shoulder, cut into
    chunks
1 pound hot sausage
2 cans (4 ounces each) green chilies, cut
    into strips
½ pound mushrooms, sliced
½ teaspoon salt
1 tablespoon anise seed
½ gallon red wine
8 large potatoes, peeled
Butter
Bread Crumbs

Cut the salt pork into strips and line the bottom of a large, heavy kettle. Layer the carrots, bay leaves, parsley, figs, onions, stew beef, pork, sausage, chili strips, and sliced mushrooms in the kettle. Combine the salt, anise seed, and wine and pour over the stew. Bring to a boil and simmer gently for 3 hours. Refrigerate overnight. Remove the stew from the refrigerator and let sit at room temperature for 3 hours. Preheat the oven to 400°F. Roll the peeled potatoes in butter and toss in bread crumbs. Wrap each potato in foil. Place in the oven along with the stew and bake 1¼ hours at 400°F. Remove the potatoes, open the foil wrappers, and return to the oven and bake until they are lightly browned, about 15 minutes. To serve, ladle the stew over the crisp potatoes.

SERVES 8.

Beef-Potato Purée-Stew

> 2 pounds beef bottom round, cubed
> 3 tablespoons all-purpose flour
> 3 tablespoons shortening
> 1 large potato, peeled and chopped
> 2 teaspoons salt
> ¼ teaspoon pepper
> 1 cup red wine
> 3 cups condensed beef bouillon
> 2 cups water
> 12 small white onions, peeled
> 2 cups yellow turnips, peeled and diced
> 6 carrots, scraped and cut into chunks
> 4 medium-sized potatoes, peeled and
>   quartered
>   Salt and pepper to taste

Dredge the meat with the flour and brown on all sides in the shortening in a large kettle. Add the chopped potato, salt, pepper, wine, bouillon, and water. Bring to a boil, cover, and simmer 1½ hours, until the meat is almost tender and the potato is reduced to a purée. Add the onions, turnips, carrots, and potatoes and simmer another 45 minutes, until the vegetables are tender. Season and serve.

SERVES 6.

Lamb-Potato Purée-Stew

2½ pounds lamb shoulder, boned
1 large onion, chopped
1 large potato, peeled and chopped
2 celery stalks, diced
1 garlic clove, minced
1 teaspoon salt
¼ teaspoon pepper
½ cup white wine
Water
18 small white onions, peeled
3 large potatoes, peeled and diced
6 small carrots, scraped and diced
1 package (10 ounces) frozen peas

Cut the lamb into 2-inch cubes and place in a heavy pot with the onion, potato, celery, garlic, salt, and pepper. Add the wine and enough water to cover the vegetables ½ inch. Bring to a boil, skim, and turn down the heat. Simmer 50 minutes, until the potato is puréed. Remove the meat. Put the liquid through a strainer and force as much of the stewed vegetables through as possible. Return the meat and liquid to the pot and correct the seasoning. Place the small white onions, potatoes, and carrots on top of the meat and cover. Simmer until the vegetables are tender, adding the peas about 6 minutes before serving.

SERVES 4 TO 6.

Lamb and Potato Jumble

    4 lamb necks, sliced about 1 inch thick
    2 tablespoons vegetable oil
    2 cups water
    ½ cup bourbon
    4 beef bouillon cubes
    8 small potatoes, peeled and halved
    ¾ teaspoon salt
    ¼ teaspoon pepper
    4 small carrots, scraped and diced
    ½ cup celery, chopped
    1 medium-sized onion, chopped
    ¼ pound mushrooms, sliced
    2 medium-sized tomatoes, cut into
        wedges
    ¼ cup chopped parsley

Cook the lamb in the oil in a Dutch oven over a low heat until browned. Add the water, bourbon, bouillon cubes, potatoes, salt, and pepper. Bring to a boil and then reduce the heat. Cover and simmer 20 minutes. Add the remaining ingredients, cover, and cook another 20 minutes, until the lamb and vegetables are tender.

SERVES 4.

Kentucky Burgoo

2 pounds pork shank
2 pounds veal shank
2 pounds beef shank
1 stewing chicken (4 pounds), cut up
8 quarts cold water
2 pounds potatoes, peeled and sliced
1½ pounds medium-sized onions, peeled
     and cut up
1 bunch carrots, scraped and diced
2 green peppers, cleaned and chopped
2 cups cabbage, chopped
1 quart tomato juice
2 cups canned whole-kernel corn
2 teaspoons chili powder
2 cups diced okra
  Chopped parsley
2 cups canned lima beans
1 cup diced celery
  Salt and pepper to taste
¼ teaspoon Tabasco sauce

Put the various meats into cold water and slowly bring to a boil. Simmer the meats until they are tender enough to fall from the bones. Lift the meat out of the broth, cool, and remove from the bones. Chop up the meats and return to the broth. Add all the vegetables and seasonings to the meat and broth. Simmer several hours until the broth is thick.

SERVES 12.

Venison Ragout

2 pounds venison stew meat, cut into
1-inch cubes
1 cup all-purpose flour
4 ounces butter or margarine
Salt and pepper to taste
½ cup Cognac
2 cups beef bouillon
1 bay leaf
2 celery stalks, chopped
½ teaspoon sage
6 small onions, peeled
¼ teaspoon powdered cloves
3 carrots, scraped and sliced
12 small potatoes, peeled
¼ pound button mushrooms

Roll the venison in the flour. Melt the butter or magarine in a pot and brown the meat on all sides. Sprinkle with salt and pepper. Add the Cognac and simmer 10 minutes. Add the bouillon, bay leaf, celery, and sage. Cover and simmer 90 minutes. Add the onions, cloves, carrots, potatoes, and mushrooms. Cover and simmer 30 minutes longer, until the meat is tender and the vegetables are done. If the liquid becomes too thick, add more bouillon. Serve the ragout in a tureen.

SERVES 4.

9

THE POTATO IN A SUPPORTING ROLE

The versatile potato probably reaches its culinary peak in the side dishes, where it is supposed to play second fiddle to a meat or fish dish. If prepared well, however, the spud can steal the show from a pedestrian roast or grilled offering. Given a little time and thought, a potato creation can turn a pick-me-up meal into a memorable repast.

It is in this supporting role that the potato has emerged in some of its famous costumes. Fried it has become a household word as Potatoes Lyonnaise, almost a meal in itself. And the crisp, buttery Rosti from Switzerland is becoming more and more popular in this country. Baked, the spud made a name for itself with the pungent Flamande and that noble invention known as Pommes Anna. And boiled we have a host of desirable dishes, including the classic Pommes de Terre à la Duchesse and the tangy, pastalike Gnocchi.

Hundreds of dishes have been dreamed up over the years—many by American cooks, a great number by the French, of course, and some from other parts of the world. It proves once more how many images this homely looking vegetable can project and how glamorous it can be.

Potatoes Flamande

    3 tablespoons finely chopped onion
  10 juniper berries, crushed
    1 teaspoon crushed garlic
  ¾ cup butter
    6 large potatoes, baked and halved
  ¼ teaspoon cayenne
      Salt and pepper to taste
      Chopped parsley

In a skillet, sauté the onion, juniper berries, and crushed garlic in the butter until the onion is soft. Scoop out the pulp from the potato halves and reserve the shells. Purée the pulp and blend in the butter mixture. Season with cayenne, salt, and pepper. Mound in the potato shells, sprinkle with chopped parsley, and serve.

SERVES 6.

Stuffing Balls

    3 onions, chopped
  ⅓ cup chopped parsley
  ½ teaspoon oregano
      Pepper to taste
    3 cups prepared herb bread stuffing
    3 cups potatoes, peeled, cooked, and
          mashed
    1 egg, beaten
    1 tablespoon water

Combine the onions, parsley, oregano, and pepper. Add 2 cups of the bread stuffing to the mashed potatoes and blend with a fork. With hands, shape this mixture into 1 inch balls. With a rolling pin, crumble the remaining bread stuffing. Combine the beaten egg with the water. Lightly coat the potato balls with the egg mixture and then the bread stuffing. Place the balls on a buttered cookie sheet and bake 20 minutes in a preheated 375°F oven.

SERVES 6 TO 8.

Rutabaga Potatoes

3 large potatoes, baked
4 cups puréed rutabagas, cooked
3 tablespoons minced onion
6 tablespoons butter
¼ cup heavy cream
2 tablespoons grated Romano cheese
Salt, paprika, and mace to taste
1 cup dried bread crumbs
Butter

Halve the potatoes and scoop out the pulp, reserving the shells. Purée the potato pulp and combine with the puréed rutabaga. In a skillet sauté the onion in the butter and stir into the puréed vegetables. Add the cream cheese, salt, paprika, and mace. Heap the mixture into the potato shells, sprinkle with bread crumbs, and dot with butter. Heat the stuffed potatoes in a preheated 375°F oven 15 minutes.

SERVES 6.

Pommes de Terre Purée

½ cup milk, scalded
5 tablespoons softened butter
2 pounds potatoes, peeled, cooked, and
    mashed
¼ teaspoon nutmeg
¼ teaspoon paprika
½ teaspoon salt
- Butter
  Paprika

Add the milk and butter to the mashed potatoes along with the nutmeg, paprika, and salt. Transfer the potatoes to a heated serving dish, add a dot of butter, sprinkle paprika atop, and serve hot.

SERVES 6.

The Potato Board was formed by an act of Congress in 1971. It is a national, nonprofit organization, funded by the potato growers of the United States. Representing both the fresh and processed United States potato industry, its objective is to eliminate misconceptions surrounding the potato—it really can be eaten while on a diet!—and to educate consumers about the virtues of tubers. The organization's educational, advertising, and promotional programs are directed toward teachers, nutritionists, doctors, and restauranteurs, as well as consumers in general. For more information, write to:

The Potato Board
1385 South Colorado Boulevard
Suite 512
Denver, Colorado 80222

Pommes Anna

3 pounds potatoes, peeled and thinly
   sliced
¼ pound butter
   Salt, pepper, and paprika to taste

In the bottom of a large cast-iron skillet, arrange circles of overlapping potato slices, alternating the direction with each row. Dot each layer with butter and sprinkle with salt, pepper, and paprika. Cover with another layer of potatoes and butter and season the same way. Arrange several overlapping layers of potatoes around the edge of the pan. Continue heaping layers until all the potatoes are used. Butter the top layer and press the potatoes down with a piece of buttered foil. Secure the foil on the pan and bake in a preheated 425°F oven 25 minutes. Remove the foil and press the potatoes down in the center with a spatula. Cook the potatoes 20 minutes more, until they are tender and browned on top. Remove the pan from the oven and let the potatoes rest 2 minutes. Shake the pan well to loosen the potatoes on the bottom. Hold the potatoes down firmly with a pan lid and pour off the excess butter. Invert the pan onto a hot serving plate, carefully removing the pan from the browned cake of potatoes.

SERVES 6 TO 8.

Among the countless nicknames for the potato are spud, tater, Mickie, Murphy, tuber, and ground apple.

Pommes de Terre Dauphinois (Scalloped)

    3 garlic cloves, split
    2½ pounds potatoes, peeled and thinly
        sliced
      Salt and paprika to taste
    ½ teaspoon thyme
    1 cup light cream
    1 ounce bourbon

Rub a baking dish with the split garlic cloves. Add layers of potatoes, overlapping slices, and sprinkle each layer with salt, paprika, and thyme. Mix the cream and bourbon, bring to a boil, and pour over the potatoes, barely covering them. Bake in a preheated 375°F oven until the potatoes are tender and delicate in color.

SERVES 6 TO 8.

Rosti

    6 tablespoons butter
    4 large potatoes, peeled, boiled, and
        coarsely grated
    1 medium-sized onion, grated
    1 cup Gruyère cheese, grated
      Salt to taste

In each of two 8-inch skillets, place 3 tablespoons butter. Divide the potatoes evenly between the pans and blend with the butter. Sprinkle the onion and cheese atop. Press the potatoes down in the pans and cook over a medium-high heat until browned on the bottom. Turn the potato cakes carefully and brown the other sides. Turn the cakes out onto hot plates and season with salt.

SERVES 4.

Potato Gnocchi

7 medium-sized potatoes, peeled and
    boiled
1 cup all-purpose flour
2 teaspoons Italian seasoning
    Boiling salted water
2 cups tomato sauce, heated
¼ teaspoon Tabasco sauce
2 tablespoons grated Romano cheese

Mash the potatoes until smooth. Put them on a floured board and mix with the flour and Italian seasoning. Use enough flour to make a dough that can be kneaded. Roll the dough into a finger-thin roll and cut into 2-inch pieces. Press each piece lightly with a fork. Drop about 20 at a time into a boiling salted water. When they come to the surface, remove from water and place in a serving dish. Keep the water boiling and repeat until all the pieces are cooked. Mix with tomato sauce seasoned with Tabasco sauce and sprinkle with cheese.

SERVES 4 TO 6.

Sour Cream Potatoes

4 medium-sized potatoes, peeled and cut
　　into ¾-inch cubes
1 small onion, minced
1 teaspoon salt
¼ teaspoon pepper
⅛ teaspoon Tabasco sauce
½ cup boiling water
¼ cup dairy sour cream
　Paprika

Put the potatoes in a skillet with the onion, salt, pepper, Tabasco sauce, and boiling water. Bring to a boil, cover, and simmer 15 minutes, until the potatoes are tender. Do not drain. Add the sour cream and toss lightly with a fork. Put in a hot serving dish and sprinkle with paprika.

SERVES 4.

Potato Mounds Amandine

1½ pounds potatoes, peeled and cut into
　　pieces
　Boiling salted water
¼ cup butter
¼ cup hot milk
　Dash almond extract
1 egg
⅛ teaspoon nutmeg
　Salt and pepper to taste
¼ cup slivered almonds

Cook the potato pieces in the boiling salted water until tender. Drain and force through a ricer. Add 2 tablespoons of the butter, the milk, almond extract, egg, and nutmeg. Season with salt and pepper. Drop from a spoon in 12 mounds on a greased cookie sheet. Melt the remaining butter, mix with the almonds, and sprinkle on the mounds. Bake in a preheated 400°F oven 15 minutes or until lightly browned.

SERVES 4.

Potatoes O'Brien

1 pound potatoes, peeled and diced
¼ cup vegetable oil
1 medium-sized onion, finely chopped
4 whole pimientos, chopped
1 medium-sized green pepper, chopped
  Salt and pepper to taste
  Paprika to taste

In a skillet, sauté the potato pieces in vegetable oil until brown and tender. Add the onion, pimientos, green pepper, salt, and pepper. When the green pepper is tender, turn out onto a serving dish and sprinkle with paprika.

SERVES 4.

Pommes Bordeaux

1 clove garlic
2 tablespoons vegetable oil
2 tomatoes, diced
½ cup diced celery
¼ teaspoon salt
¼ teaspoon pepper
¼ teaspoon ground rosemary
4 medium-sized potatoes, peeled, boiled,
    and thinly sliced

In a skillet, brown the garlic lightly in the oil and remove. Add the tomatoes, celery, salt, pepper, and rosemary. Cook gently 5 minutes. Add the potatoes and cook 10 minutes longer.

SERVES 4.

Pommes de Terre à la Duchesse

2 pounds potatoes, peeled, quartered,
    and boiled
½ cup butter
½ teaspoon salt
⅛ teaspoon Tabasco sauce
¼ teaspoon paprika
1 egg yolk

Drain the water off of the potatoes and let them dry. Mash well. Add the butter, salt, Tabasco sauce, and paprika and mix well over a low heat, stirring until smooth. Remove from the heat, add the egg yolk, and mix well about 5 minutes, if possible in the top of a double boiler to retain heat.

SERVES 4 TO 6.

Pommes à l'Ardennaise
by Hans Durst

Hans Durst is executive chef at Houston's Warwick Hotel, which is widely known for its continental cuisine. Durst served his apprenticeship under noted chefs in West Germany. He is a member of Les Amis d'Escoffier Society.

4 Idaho potatoes, baked
1 egg yolk
2 tablespoons butter
3 ounces Westphalian or prosciutto ham, diced
¼ cup canned mushrooms, finely chopped
  Salt, pepper, and nutmeg to taste
1 tablespoon grated Parmesan cheese

Cut the potatoes in half, crosswise, and trim off the base of each half, so that they can stand up. Using a teaspoon, remove the potato pulp, reserving the shells. Combine the potato pulp with the remaining ingredients except the cheese. Stuff the potato shells with the filling mixture, using a pastry tube if desired. Make small stars around the edges of the potato halves. Continue filling each half in the shape of a cone. Sprinkle with cheese and place in a preheated 350°F oven until the cheese melts.

SERVES 8.

Galette

 5 medium-sized potatoes, peeled, diced,
    and boiled
½ cup butter
 1 cup beef consommé
 1 ounce dry sherry
   Salt and pepper to taste
 2 medium-sized onions, chopped
⅛ teaspoon powdered mace

Mash the potatoes while still warm. Put the potatoes in a pot, preferably the top of a double boiler, and mix in 4 tablespoons of the butter, the consommé, and the sherry. Season with salt and pepper, stirring all the time. In another pan, lightly brown the onions in 2 tablespoons of the butter. Add the potatoes and mix well. Add the mace after the mixture is removed from heat. Put into a 1-quart baking dish and dot with the remaining butter. Bake in a preheated 400°F oven until a brown crust forms.

SERVES 4.

Delmonico Potatoes

 2 pounds potatoes, cooked, peeled, and
    sliced
 4 hard-cooked eggs, sliced
 1 tablespoon butter
 1 tablespoon flour
½ cup milk
 1 cup grated cheddar cheese
   Cayenne

Alternate layers of potatoes and sliced eggs in individual casseroles. Melt the butter and add the flour and milk. Pour a little of the sauce over each serving, sprinkle with cheese, and dust with cayenne. Bake in a preheated 350°F oven 15 minutes.

SERVES 4.

Stuffed Potato Balls

by Ira Ernest Dole

Ira Ernest Dole is executive chef at one of the best-known hotels in the West, the Brown Palace of Denver, Colorado.

  1 pound lean pork
  1 small tomato
  1 medium-sized onion
  1 tablespoon vegetable oil
  ¼ teaspoon oregano
  ½ teaspoon salt
  ¼ teaspoon pepper
  2 teaspoons chopped parsley
  4 eggs, beaten
12 large Idaho potatoes, steamed, peeled, and mashed
  Fat for deep frying

Grind the pork, tomato, and onion in a food chopper, using a medium blade. Cook this mixture in oil in a heavy frying pan about 15 minutes, or until the pork loses its pink color. Combine the seasonings, parsley, and eggs with the potatoes and knead to make a dough. Make balls with 3 tablespoons of the potato dough. Fill each potato ball with 1 teaspoon of the meat mixture, shaping it like a football. Repeat until all the dough and filling are used. Fry the balls in deep fat at 375°F 4 to 5 minutes, until golden brown. Serve hot.

SERVES 12.

Swirled Whipped Potatoes

Water
1½ pounds white potatoes (about 5
     medium-sized), peeled and
     quartered
1½ pounds sweet potatoes, peeled and
     quartered
 2 teaspoons salt
½ cup butter
½ cup light cream
¼ teaspoon pepper

In 2 large, tightly covered saucepans in 1 inch of water, cook the white potatoes and sweet potatoes separately with 1 teaspoon salt each until tender, 15 to 20 minutes for the white potatoes and 10 to 15 minutes for the sweet potatoes. With an electric mixer at medium-high speed, beat the white potatoes until they are fluffy. Beat in ¼ cup of the butter, ¼ cup of the light cream, and ⅛ teaspoon pepper. Repeat with the sweet potatoes, using the remaining ingredients. Spoon the white potatoes and sweet potatoes alternately into a glass baking dish to create a marbled appearance. Bake in a preheated 375°F oven 40 minutes, until heated through.

SERVES 10.

Hasselback Potatoes

6 medium-sized potatoes (about 2
     pounds) peeled
 Melted butter
 Salt and pepper to taste
¼ cup dry bread crumbs

Rest a potato in the bowl of a large spoon and slice downward, but not entirely through, at ¼-inch intervals, starting ½ inch from the end. Repeat with the remaining potatoes. Place the potatoes, cut sides up, in a baking dish. Brush with melted butter. Bake in a preheated 425°F oven 30 minutes. Remove from the oven and brush again with more melted butter. Season with salt, pepper, and bread crumbs. Bake 20 to 30 minutes more or until golden.

SERVES 6.

Potatoes Lyonnaise

6 medium-sized potatoes (about 2
   pounds)
  Boiling salted water
6 tablespoons butter
2 medium-sized onions, thinly sliced
  Salt and pepper
2 tablespoons chopped parsley

Cook the potatoes, covered, in 1 inch of boiling salted water until tender, about 30 minutes. Drain, peel, and slice ¼ inch thick. In a large skillet over a medium-high heat, melt 3 tablespoons of the butter. Add the sliced potatoes and cook until brown on both sides, turning frequently with a spatula. In another skillet, melt the remaining 3 tablespoons of butter. Cook the onions slowly over a medium-low heat until tender, stirring occasionally. Combine the onions and potatoes and season with salt and pepper. Turn into a heated serving bowl and garnish with parsley.

SERVES 6.

Cheese-Stuffed Baked Potatoes

    6 medium-sized potatoes (about 2
        pounds)
    1 large-sized package (8 ounces) cream
        cheese, softened
    ½ cup soft butter
    1 tablespoon chopped green onion
    ½ teaspoon salt
        Dash pepper
        Paprika to taste

Bake the potatoes in a preheated 400°F oven 45 minutes or until tender. Remove from oven and knead gently. Cut a piece off the top of each potato and scoop the pulp from the shell. Reserve the shells. With a fork, mash the pulp. Blend in the cream cheese, butter, onion, salt, and pepper. Fill the potato shells with the mixture. Sprinkle with paprika. Reheat at 400°F 15 to 20 minutes.

SERVES 6.

Potatoes with Sauce Verte

    4 cups instant mashed potato flakes
    4 cups boiling water
        Salt and pepper to taste
    1 pound fresh mushrooms
    1 cup soft butter
    1 cup mayonnaise
    1 egg
    ¼ cup watercress, chopped
    ¼ cup parsley, chopped
    2 teaspoons tarragon
    2 green onions, chopped

Stir the potatoes into boiling water and season with salt and pepper. Butter a 6-cup mold with about half of the butter. Slice some of the larger mushrooms, cook in a little butter, and press around the sides and top of the mold. Chop the rest of the mushrooms and cook in the remaining butter. Pack the potatoes about halfway in the mold. Spread the chopped mushrooms in a layer, and top with the rest of the potatoes. Bake in a preheated 350°F oven until hot. To make the green sauce, combine the rest of the ingredients in a blender. Unmold the potatoes and cover with the green sauce.

SERVES 8.

Potato Quenelles

    3 medium-sized potatoes (about 1
        pound)
     Salted water
    2 eggs
    ⅛ teaspoon nutmeg
       Salt and pepper to taste
    ¾ cup flour
       Melted butter
       Chopped parsley

Cook the potatoes, covered, in 1 inch of boiling salted water until tender, about 35 minutes. Drain, peel, and mash to make 2 cups mashed potatoes. Beat in the eggs, nutmeg, salt, and pepper. Stir in the flour; the mixture will be soft. Shape the potato mixture into ovals with a teaspoon or force through a pastry bag using the rosette tip. (Dip the spoon into hot water between shaping the ovals; they will slide off of the spoon more easily.) In a saucepan half-filled with simmering salted water, poach the quenelles about 5 minutes. Remove with a slotted spoon to a buttered heat-proof serving dish. Drizzle melted butter over them and sprinkle with parsley. Serve hot.

SERVES 8.

Potato Kugel

    3 eggs
    3 cups potatoes, peeled and grated
    ⅓ cup flour
    ½ teaspoon baking powder
        Salt and pepper to taste
    1 small grated onion
    ¼ cup chicken fat or melted butter

Beat the eggs until thick and light. To wring moisture from the potatoes, wrap them tightly in a towel and twist each end in opposite directions. Add the potatoes to the eggs along with the flour, baking powder, salt, pepper, onion, and chicken fat or melted butter. Bake in a buttered 1½-quart casserole in a preheated 350°F oven 1 hour, until golden brown.

SERVES 6.

Delmonico Potato Torte

    6 tablespoons butter
    6 medium-sized potatoes, peeled and
        thinly sliced
    1 cup grated Parmesan cheese
        Salt and pepper to taste
    ½ teaspoon nutmeg
    ½ cup grated Gruyère or Swiss cheese
    ¼ cup heavy cream
    2 tablespoons freeze-dried chives

Grease a 2-quart mold or heat-proof bowl with the butter. Layer the potatoes in the mold or bowl, sprinkling each layer with Parmesan cheese, salt, pepper, and nutmeg. Cover tightly with a lid or foil. Bake in a preheated 400°F oven until the potatoes are done, about 1 hour. Unmold into a serving dish. Sprinkle with cheese and brown quickly under the broiler. Pour the cream slowly into the center of the potatoes. Sprinkle with chives.

SERVES 6.

Potato Rosti
by Dieter Paul

Dieter Paul, who attended a special chef's school in Germany for four years, is executive chef at the Fairmont Hotel in Dallas, Texas.

```
 6 pounds large Idaho potatoes
   Salted water
 1 cup corn oil
   Salt and pepper to taste
12 slices bacon, diced
 3 cups chopped white onion
½ cup chopped parsley
```

Wash the potatoes and boil them in salted water 12 to 15 minutes, until semisoft. Peel and put into the refrigerator to cool. Grate the potatoes on a coarse grater. Fry the grated potatoes in the corn oil on a griddle. Add the salt and pepper. When golden brown, turn the potatoes with a spatula and brown the other side. For each serving, sauté a little bacon and onion in a skillet and cook until the onion is transparent. Add enough potatoes for 1 portion and blend. Shape the potatoes, bacon, and onion like a pancake and fry over a medium heat until golden brown, about 5 minutes. When ready, put a plate upside down on the skillet and turn over the pan. Repeat until all the potatoes, bacon, and onion are used. Sprinkle with chopped parsley.

SERVES 12.

Cattle King Potatoes

½ pound sliced mushrooms in butter
3 pounds potatoes, peeled
  Boiling water
1 teaspoon salt
2 cloves garlic
⅓ cup butter
2 egg yolks
½ cup light cream
  Salt and pepper to taste
¼ cup chopped parsley

Sauté the mushrooms in butter. Cook the potatoes until tender in boiling water with the salt and garlic cloves. Mash the potatoes well and mix in the butter, egg yolks, and cream. Season with salt and pepper. Fold in the mushrooms and parsley. Keep warm in a low oven until ready to serve.

SERVES 8.

10

THE POTATO AS A SWEET

The final course of the meal is the dessert, unless you count nibbling walnuts with your port as a course, and in many households it is given equal billing with the entrée. The word *dessert* comes from the French verb *desservir*—which means "to clear away"; and that's just what you do before bringing on the cake, pie, or pudding.

It may seem incongruous to write about desserts in a potato cookbook, but there is a surprising range of sweets in which the spud is an ingredient. Most famous perhaps is the rich potato chocolate cake which used to be a center of attraction at basket socials, ladies' club luncheons, and church suppers around the turn of the century. Food writer James Beard thought enough of this goodie to describe it as the most elevated use of the potato. But there are other succulent sweets, ranging from Spiced Potato Cookies to tangy Potato-Almond Pudding, that should delight the most demanding dessert buff.

Mashed Potato Chocolate Cake I

1 cup soft butter
2 cups sugar
4 eggs
2 squares unsweetened chocolate, melted
1 teaspoon vanilla
1 cup cold mashed potatoes
2 cups sifted flour
1 teaspoon baking soda
1 teaspoon salt
¾ cup sour milk or buttermilk

Preheat the oven to 375°F. In the large bowl of an electric mixer, cream together at a medium-high speed the butter and sugar. Beat in the eggs, one at a time, along with the melted chocolate and vanilla until blended. Reduce the speed, stir in the potatoes, and mix well. Onto waxed paper, sift together the flour, baking soda, and salt. Add the dry ingredients to the batter alternately with the sour milk or buttermilk, blending well after each addition. Pour into 3 greased 9-inch cake pans (or one 9-inch tube pan). Bake the 9-inch layers 20 minutes (or the 9-inch tube pan 1 hour) or until a cake tester inserted in the center comes out clean. Cool the cake 10 minutes in the pans and then remove the cake from the pans to wire racks to cool completely. Fill and frost the cake with your favorite frosting.

SERVES 10.

Potato Chocolate Cake II

      6 ounces soft butter
 1½ cups sugar
      4 eggs, separated
      1 cup hot potatoes, riced
 1½ cups sifted all-purpose flour
      2 teaspoons baking powder
      ½ teaspoon salt
      ½ cup cocoa
      ½ teaspoon powdered mace
      ¼ teaspoon ground cloves
      1 ounce crème de cacao
      1 cup milk
      1 teaspoon vanilla
      1 cup pitted dates, chopped
      Chocolate Potato Frosting

Cream the butter and 1 cup of the sugar until light. Add the egg yolks and beat well. Add the potatoes and mix thoroughly. Sift together the dry ingredients and add to the creamed butter alternately with the crème de cacao and milk, beating until smooth. Add the vanilla and dates. Beat the egg whites until stiff but not dry. Gradually add the remaining sugar to the whites, beating until very stiff. Fold the egg whites into the cake batter. Pour the mixture into a pan (13- by 9- by 2-inches) lined on the bottom with waxed paper. Bake in a preheated 350°F oven about 45 minutes. Cool and frost with the Chocolate Potato Frosting.

SERVES 6 TO 8.

Chocolate Potato Frosting

⅓ cup butter
2 ounces unsweetened chocolate
⅓ cup cooked potatoes, riced
⅛ teaspoon salt
1½ teaspoons vanilla
¼ teaspoon cinnamon
1 egg
3 cups confectioners' sugar
1 tablespoon milk

In a small saucepan, melt the butter and chocolate over a low heat. Remove from the heat. Beat in the potatoes, salt, vanilla, and cinnamon. Beat in the egg, confectioners' sugar, and milk. Continue beating until the frosting is of spreading consistency.

In the United States, the use of potatoes for spirits has become minimal. But in Germany, potatoes are used to make schnapps; in Russia, they are distilled into vodka.

Potato Chocolate Cake III

⅓ cup margarine
1½ cups sugar
4 eggs
1 cup mashed potatoes
½ cup milk
2 cups cake flour
6 tablespoons cocoa
1 tablespoon baking powder
1 teaspoon cinnamon
1 teaspoon nutmeg
½ teaspoon salt

In the large bowl of an electric mixer cream together at a medium-high speed the margarine and sugar. Add the eggs one at a time, beating well after each addition. Beat in the potatoes. In a separate bowl mix the cake flour, cocoa, baking powder, cinnamon, nutmeg, and salt. Alternately add the dry ingredients and milk to the beaten mixture. Beat 2 minutes. Line two 8- or 9-inch round cake pans with waxed paper cut to fit the bottoms. Pour half of the batter into each pan. Bake in a preheated 350°F oven 45 minutes, until a cake tester inserted in the center comes out clean. Cool the cakes in the pans 15 minutes and then invert them onto wire racks to cool completely. Sprinkle with confectioner's sugar or frost with the Chocolate Potato Frosting.

SERVES 16.

Potato Pecan Surprises

½ cup soft butter or margarine
1 cup confectioners' sugar
¼ cup cold mashed potatoes
2 tablespoons milk
1 teaspoon vanilla
¼ teaspoon salt
1¾ cups sifted flour
1 cup chopped pecans

Preheat the oven to 350°F. In the large bowl of an electric mixer cream together at a medium-high speed the butter and ½ of the cup confectioner's sugar. Add the mashed potatoes, milk, vanilla, and salt and mix well. With a wooden spoon, stir in the flour and pecans until blended. Shape into 1-inch balls. Bake at 350°F on a greased cookie sheet about 20 minutes. Cool slightly and roll them in the remaining confectioners' sugar.

MAKES 3 DOZEN COOKIES.

Mock Marzipan with Raisins

1 cup California raisins
½ teaspoon almond extract
1 medium-sized potato, boiled and
  peeled
2 packages (1 pound each) confectioners'
  sugar
½ cup ground almonds
  Dried apricots
  Pitted prunes
  Pitted dates
  Dried figs
  Shelled and chopped nuts

Arrange the raisins in one layer in a jelly-roll pan. Freeze them. When hard, finely chop the raisins in a blender set at high speed. Set aside. In the small bowl of an electric mixer, beat at high speed the almond extract and potato until smooth. With hands, knead in the confectioners' sugar, a little at a time, to make a stiff dough. Knead in the raisins and almonds. Refrigerate in a tightly covered jar until ready to use. To prepare the candies, allow the dough to stand at room temperature until soft. Use to stuff dried fruits (apricots, prunes, dates, or figs), sandwich between nut halves, or roll into balls and coat with chopped nuts.

MAKES 2½ CUPS.

Spud Bars

2 tablespoons butter
½ cup granulated sugar
¼ cup brown sugar, packed
½ cup flour
½ teaspoon baking soda
¼ teaspoon salt
¼ teaspoon cinnamon
1 egg
1 teaspoon vanilla
½ cup potato granules

In the large bowl of an electric mixer, cream together at a medium-high speed the butter, granulated sugar, and brown sugar. Beat in the flour, baking soda, salt, and cinnamon until well blended. With a spatula, stir in the egg and vanilla and then the potato granules. Pour the batter into a nonstick 8-inch-square baking pan. Bake in a preheated 350°F oven 20 minutes. Remove from the pan and cut while still slightly warm.

MAKES 16 TWO-INCH SQUARES.

Apple Crisp

2 apples, peeled and sliced
⅓ cup potato granules
2 tablespoons granulated sugar
3 tablespoons brown sugar
¼ teaspoon cinnamon
1 tablespoon butter

Arrange the apple slices in a nonstick 8-inch-square baking pan. In a small bowl, combine the potato granules, granulated sugar, brown sugar, and cinnamon. With a pastry blender, cut in the butter. Sprinkle the mixture over the apples. Bake, uncovered, in a preheated 375°F oven 25 minutes or until the apples are tender.

SERVES 4.

Spiced Potato Cookies

⅔ cup soft butter
1¾ cups sugar
4 eggs
¼ teaspoon almond extract
1 cup warm mashed potatoes
2 cups flour
3 teaspoons baking powder
1 teaspoon ginger
1 teaspoon powdered mace
½ teaspoon allspice
½ teaspoon salt
1 cup chopped almonds
Spicy white sugar icing, optional

Cream the butter with the sugar until the mixture is as smooth as possible. Beat in the eggs, almond extract, and mashed potatoes thoroughly. Sift together the flour, baking powder, ginger, mace, allspice, and salt. Stir the spiced flour gradually into the potato mixture and add the chopped almonds. Drop the batter from a teaspoon onto lightly oiled cookie sheets, placing the mounds about 2 inches apart. Bake the cookies in a preheated 375°F oven 12 minutes or until they are light brown. Remove the cookies to a wire rack and let cool. If desired, top the cookies with a spicy white sugar icing.

MAKES ABOUT 3 DOZEN COOKIES.

Potato-Carrot Pudding

1 cup grated raw potatoes
1 teaspoon baking soda
1 cup grated raw carrots
1 cup sugar
1 cup flour
1 cup raisins
1 egg, well beaten
2 tablespoons melted butter
1 tablespoon Cognac
1 teaspoon salt
½ teaspoon white pepper
½ teaspoon ginger
½ teaspoon ground nutmeg
    Whipped cream or custard sauce,
        optional

In a bowl, mix the potatoes and baking soda. In a second bowl, combine all the other ingredients. Combine the two mixtures and pour the batter into a buttered baking dish. Put the dish into a pan of hot water and bake the pudding in a preheated 350°F oven 2 hours. If the surface is getting overly browned during the baking, cover the top with foil. Let the pudding cool 15 minutes, invert the dish onto a serving platter, and unmold. If desired, top the pudding with whipped cream or a custard sauce.

SERVES 6 TO 8.

Valentine's Day Cake

2½ cups sifted flour
4 teaspoons baking powder
½ teaspoon salt
¼ teaspoon powdered mace
¾ cup shortening
2 cups sugar
2 eggs, separated
3 squares (1 ounce each) unsweetened
    chocolate, melted
1 cup mashed potatoes
1 teaspoon vanilla
¾ cup milk

FILLING

3 tablespoons cornstarch
½ cup sugar
1 cup orange juice
1 cup flaked coconut

FROSTING

2 cups of heavy cream
Flaked coconut, tinted pink

Sift together the flour, baking powder, salt, and mace. In a bowl, cream the shortening until light. Gradually add the sugar, and cream until light and fluffy. Add the egg yolks and beat well. Mix in the chocolate, potatoes, and vanilla. Blend well. Add the sifted ingredients and milk alternately to the chocolate mixture, beating well after each addition. Beat the egg whites until stiff and fold into the batter. Turn the batter into 3 greased and floured 8-inch layer cake pans. Bake in a preheated 350°F oven 40 minutes, until a cake tester shows that the cake is done.

Cool 5 minutes in the pans. Remove from the pans and cool thoroughly.

To make the Filling, mix the cornstarch and sugar in a saucepan. Slowly add the orange juice, stirring steadily. Cook over a low heat, stirring until thickened and clear. Remove from heat. Stir in the coconut flakes and cool. Spread the filling over 2 of the cake layers. Stack the layers and place the plain layer on top.

For the Frosting, whip the heavy cream well and frost the top and sides of cake. Sprinkle coconut over the top of the cake in a heart-shaped pattern. Chill the cake until serving time.

Potato-Almond Pudding

4 large Idaho potatoes, peeled
1 teaspoon salt
1 tablespoon sugar
½ cup salad oil
3 eggs, beaten
½ cup ground almonds
1 cup honey

Grate the potatoes or purée them in a blender. Drain off most of the liquid from the potatoes. Add the salt and sugar. Heat the oil in a small skillet and when it is hot, immediately add the potatoes, stirring until thoroughly blended. Beat in the eggs and ground almonds. Place the mixture in a well-greased 9- by 13- by 2-inch pan. Bake in a preheated 400°F oven about 1 hour, until done. The pudding should have a brown crust and the edges should stand away from the pan. Serve the pudding with honey.

SERVES 4 TO 6.

In Scandinavia, where the potato has seen the people through many an otherwise lean year, fondness for the spud borders on veneration, particularly in Denmark and Sweden.

The Danes were not sure what category to place the potato in when they first tasted it in the eighteenth century. So they served it hot and salted in a napkin as a dessert course! Times changed, however, and by the nineteenth century, meat and potatoes became the backbone of the Danish diet. One dish, which was a favorite of King Christian X, consists of boiled potatoes bathed in a gravy made with salt pork.

The dessert image of the spud apparently still persists in Denmark. Christmas dinner features roast goose, red cabbage, lingonberries, and a dish called brunede kartofler, which consists of boiled new potatoes coated with hot caramelized sugar.

Sweden's respect for the potato stems from the great famine of 1771-72, when that discovery from the New World made its first appearance on the tables of the masses. It had become known in Sweden after Swedish soldiers who had served in Prussia returned home with praise for this robust new vegetable. At last the Swedes had something to fall back on during years of crop failures. To this day, many Swedes still eat potatoes at both lunch and dinner. In fact, the tuber has been described as the frame around the Swedish meal. One favorite in that land is rarakor, which consists of grated raw potatoes, seasoned with salt, pepper, and chives and dropped a couple of tablespoons at a time into a greased frying pan. The result is a thin, crunchy, golden lace.

Orange Potato Loaf

2¾ cups sifted all-purpose flour
1 cup sugar
2½ teaspoons baking powder
1 teaspoon baking soda
¾ teaspoon salt
1 egg, beaten
1 tablespoon salad oil
1¼ cups fresh orange juice
1 tablespoon grated fresh orange rind
½ teaspoon vanilla
⅔ cup cooked potatoes, riced
½ cup chopped walnuts

In a large bowl, sift together the flour, sugar, baking powder, baking soda, and salt. In a small bowl, beat together the egg, oil, orange juice, orange rind, and vanilla. Stir in the riced potatoes. Add the orange mixture to the dry ingredients in the large bowl and mix well. Stir in the walnuts. Turn into a greased 9- by 5- by 3-inch loaf pan. Bake in a preheated 325°F oven 60 to 65 minutes, until a cake tester inserted into the loaf comes out clean. Cool 10 minutes in the pan and then remove from the pan to cool completely.

MAKES 1 LOAF.

Southern Yule Cake

2 cups sifted all-purpose flour
4 teaspoons baking powder
1 teaspoon ground cloves
½ teaspoon cinnamon
1 cup butter
2 cups sugar
2 egg yolks
1 cup mashed potatoes, whipped
½ cup milk
½ cup raisins
1 tablespoon bourbon
2 egg whites

Butter and line the bottom of a 9- by 13-inch baking pan with waxed paper. Sift the flour, baking powder, cloves, and cinnamon together. Cream the butter, add the sugar, and blend well. Add the egg yolks and beat until the mixture is light and fluffy. Blend in the whipped potatoes. Add the flour mixture alternately with the milk, beating until smooth after each addition. Stir in the raisins and bourbon. Beat the egg whites until stiff and gently fold into the batter. Turn into a prepared pan and bake in a preheated 350°F oven about 40 minutes, until a cake tester shows that it is done.

SERVES 10 TO 12.

11

THE POTATO AS A GOURMET DISH

Not only is the potato considered by many the most important vegetable in the world, but it has come to play a major role in haute cuisine. Once regarded solely as a cheap and easy means to keep the masses fed, the grubby, graceless spud suddenly began projecting a glamorous image after it had been accepted as a banquet item by the French court of Louis XVI and Marie Antoinette.

Toward the end of the nineteenth century, the potato had become an item on gourmet menus all over Europe. Somewhere along the way, the Swiss created their now classic Rosti, and the Italians dreamed up Gnocchi.

As famed food writer Julia Child once commented, the potato may have had humble origins, but it became one of the wonders of the gastronomical world when subjected to the imagination of the great French chefs. After all, she added, just as the French can dress up a hen's egg a thousand ways, so can they do myriad wonders with the spud. A slight exaggeration perhaps, but there are indeed plenty of potato variations. One Irish writer claimed to know four hundred. It suffices to say that the prestigious *Larousse Gastronomique*, the encyclopedia of classic French cookery, lists more than a hundred potato recipes.

The late Michael Field of food fame pointed out that the most remarkable attribute of the potato is its ability to absorb a number of flavors and still retain its character. A classic example is the luxurious Salade Françillon. This remarkable dish was the rage among fashionable Parisians in the late nineteenth century, yet few Americans today have ever heard of and much less eaten it. It was first described in *Françillon*, a play by Alexander Dumas *fils*, although it is not clear whether the salad was his invention. Salade Françillon is luxurious indeed. It calls for potatoes marinated in champagne and topped with truffles, which run about $200 a pound or more in today's market. It is a lovely dish if you have unlimited resources.

By the early twentieth century, the potato was featured on American menus in plush eating establishments such as Rector's and Delmonico's and on the wonderful Pullman diners in the days when lunch on a train consisted of something more than a sandwich and a bottle of soda pop. Dishes in those days ranged from terrapin stew on the Baltimore and Ohio to broiled sage hen on the Sante Fe. But the attraction featured on the Northern Pacific was simpler and more forthright. That railroad billed itself as the "line of the great big baked potato."

The recipes for some of the gourmet dishes mentioned here have been given in earlier chapters. Certain of the more lavish potato offerings have been selected for this section to emphasize the true gourmet potential of the spud. To begin with, a recipe is given for one of the simplest but probably the most expensive gourmet potato dishes—the heavenly combination of beluga caviar, sour cream, and baked potatoes that was once a feature aboard transoceanic luxury liners.

Caviar with Baked Potato

2 large potatoes, baked thoroughly and
  halved
Salt, *optional*

8 ounces dairy sour cream
8 ounces fresh beluga caviar

Soften the pulp of each potato half with a fork. Add salt if desired, but keep in mind that caviar has a saltiness of its own. Mix 2 ounces of the sour cream in the pulp of each potato half, keeping it inside the shell. Carefully spoon 2 ounces of caviar on the top of each potato half. Serve with ice-cold Russian or Polish vodka or chilled champagne.

SERVES 4.

Soup Vinho Verde

1 onion, chopped
2 tablespoons butter
2 tablespoons flour
2 cups water
1 large potato, peeled and diced
1 can (4⅜ ounces) Portuguese sardines,
    drained and chopped
⅛ teaspoon salt
⅛ teaspoon pepper
½ cup milk
1 ounce Vinho Verde (Portuguese white
    wine)
Croutons

In a pan, sauté the onion in the butter until very light brown. Add the flour and blend to a smooth paste. Slowly blend in the water, stirring to keep the mixture smooth. Add the potato. Simmer until the potato is soft. Add the sardines to the soup mixture. Season with salt and pepper. Add the milk and wine. Serve hot with croutons atop.

SERVES 6.

Salade Françillon

4 pounds mussels in shells
2 cups brut champagne
2 shallots, finely chopped
2 pounds small new potatoes
1 quart beef bouillon
5 ounces olive oil
2 ounces white wine vinegar
  Salt and pepper to taste
¼ teaspoon cayenne
2 tablespoons finely chopped parsley
2 tablespoons minced chives
1 can (2 ounces) black truffles, thinly
    sliced
  Lettuce

Scrub the mussels, removing the beards, and rinse them in several changes of water. Put the mussels in a kettle with 1 cup of the champagne and shallots. Cook, covered, over moderately high heat 6 minutes until the shells open. Discard any unopened shells. When the mussels are cool enough to handle, remove them from the shells. Boil the potatoes in the bouillon until tender. Drain, peel, and thinly slice. Marinate the warm potato slices in the remaining champagne for 10 minutes. Make a dressing from a mixture of the oil, vinegar, salt, and pepper. Add the cayenne and stir well. Combine the potatoes and mussels and add the dressing. Add the parsley and chives and toss the salad gently to avoid breaking the potato slices. Place in a cut crystal bowl. Scatter the truffles over the top of the salad. Cover the bowl with plastic wrap and chill 1 hour. Garnish with lettuce before serving.

SERVES 6.

Salade Niçoise

    1 pound new potatoes, peeled
    1 pound fresh string beans, diced
    5 ounces olive oil
    2 ounces lemon juice
      Salt and pepper to taste
    ¼ teaspoon cayenne
    1 cup shallots, minced
    ½ cup pitted black olives
    2 tablespoons capers
    2 hard-cooked eggs, quartered
    2 medium-sized tomatoes, quartered
    2 tablespoons chopped basil

Boil the potatoes and string beans until barely tender and chill. Make a dressing from the oil, lemon juice, salt, pepper, and cayenne and mix lightly with the potatoes and string beans. Add the shallots and toss. Mound the salad on a platter and cover with black olives and capers. Garnish with egg and tomato quarters and sprinkle with basil.

SERVES 4.

Scallop and Potato Salad in White Wine

6 potatoes, boiled and peeled
2 cups Chablis wine
1 pound scallops
2 tablespoons minced chives
2 tablespoons chopped parsley
  Mayonnaise
¼ teaspoon paprika

Cut the potatoes into slices while still warm and marinate in 1 cup of the Chablis. Poach the scallops until firm, about 10 minutes. Drain and cool. Arrange the potatoes and scallops in a salad bowl, add the chives and parsley, and toss lightly. Add the mayonnaise and toss again. Sprinkle paprika atop and serve.

SERVES 4.

Roast Beef Potato Salad in Rhine Wine

1 pound lean sliced cold roast beef, cut
    into julienne strips
2 tablespoons minced onion
2 tablespoons chopped green olives
2 potatoes, boiled, peeled, and sliced
2 medium-sized tomatoes, quartered
2 hard-cooked eggs, sliced
1 teaspoon tarragon
1 cup Rhine wine

1 cup olive oil
2 tablespoons white wine vinegar
Salt and pepper to taste
Lettuce

Put the beef in a salad bowl with the onion, olives, potatoes, tomatoes, and egg slices. Combine the tarragon, wine, oil, vinegar, salt, and pepper. Mix the dressing and pour over the salad. Chill 2 hours, dress with lettuce, and serve.

SERVES 4.

Potato-Chestnut Salad

24 small new potatoes, boiled and peeled
¼ cup shallots, chopped
2 tablespoons parsley, minced
¼ cup melted butter
¾ cup dry white wine
2 tablespoons white wine vinegar
½ cup olive oil
¾ cup whole chestnuts, cooked
½ cup green pepper, finely diced
Salt and pepper to taste
½ teaspoon paprika

While the potatoes are still warm, combine with the shallots, parsley, melted butter, and a dressing made from the wine, vinegar, and olive oil. Add the chestnuts, green pepper, salt, and pepper. Sprinkle paprika atop and chill several hours before serving.

SERVES 6 TO 8.

Portuguese Potato Salad

>2 cans (4⅜ ounces each) Portuguese
>   sardines
>½ cup dairy sour cream
>1 teaspoon prepared mustard
>1½ teaspoon pepper
>3 hard-cooked eggs
>4 cups cold cooked potatoes, diced
>1 cup celery, finely chopped
>2 tablespoons minced onions
>1 teaspoon finely chopped parsley

Mash the contents of 1 can of the sardines. Add the sour cream, mustard, and pepper. Mix thoroughly and set aside. Chop 2 of the hard-cooked eggs and mix with the potatoes. Add the celery, onions, and parsley. Mix in the sardine–sour cream dressing. Thinly slice the remaining hard-cooked egg. Drain the oil from the other can of sardines. Garnish the salad with egg slices and sardines.

SERVES 6.

Salade Pommes de Terre avec Sauternes

>1 pound small new potatoes, boiled and
>   peeled
>½ cup chopped celery
>¼ cup chopped onion
>½ cup chopped apple
>¼ cup Sauternes
>2 teaspoons dill weed
>½ cup dairy sour cream
> Salt and pepper to taste
> Paprika

Chill the potatoes and combine with the celery, onion, and apple in a salad bowl. Pour the wine over the mixture and refrigerate. Stir the salad several times while it is being chilled. Just before serving, blend the dill into the sour cream and pour over the salad, adding salt and pepper. Toss the salad gently to coat the potatoes. Sprinkle with paprika and serve.

SERVES 3 TO 4.

Growing Potatoes as House Plants

Take a firm, ripe potato with a few sprouts and cut it into four to eight pieces. Each piece should have at least one eye but no more than three. Place the pieces on a dish, allowing them to dry at room temperature for a day or so. Avoid direct sunlight as this can damage the spuds. Allow some space for air between each, and callouses will develop.

Plant one piece in an eight-inch flowerpot and cover it with one inch of soil. After a good root system develops, the stems will break through the soil. Of course, potatoes that grow in flowerpots will not be as large as those grown outdoors, but they will be a good size.

Place your potted potato in the sunniest window you have and it will soon sprout lovely yellow and white flowers resembling those of the tomato plant, to which the potato is closely related. Eventually, the flowers will be replaced by berries resembling tiny green tomatoes. These are not to be eaten.

What can be eaten, though, is below. Wash the soil away from the plant and remove the roots. You will find that your piece of potato has produced many more potatoes.

Pommes Roquefort

      6 Idaho potatoes
      ½ cup firmly packed Roquefort cheese
      ½ cup heavy cream
        Salt and pepper to taste
      ⅓ cup finely crushed French *biscotte*
          crumbs (available at delicacy shops)
      ½ clove garlic, crushed
      3 tablespoons melted butter

Scrub the potatoes and bake in a preheated 350°F oven 1 hour or until easily pierced. Slice off the tops of the potatoes and scoop out the pulp, reserving the shells. Mash the potato pulp, beating in the cheese. Gradually beat in the cream until the potatoes are light and fluffy. Season with salt and pepper. Spoon the potato mixture into the potato shells, heaping high. In a bowl, mix the *biscotte* crumbs, garlic, and butter. Sprinkle the mixture over the potatoes. Return to 350°F oven 25 minutes or until brown and crusty.

Pommes Alsacienne

      ¼ cup butter
      1 small head cabbage, cored and
          chopped coarsely
      2 large onions chopped
      6 medium-sized potatoes, boiled, peeled,
          and thinly sliced
      ¼ cup flour
      1 can (13¾ ounces) chicken broth
      2 cups grated Port Salut cheese

In a large saucepan, heat the butter and sauté the cabbage and onions until wilted. Place the cabbage, onions, and potatoes in a shallow 3-quart casserole. Stir the flour into the pan juices. Gradually stir in the chicken broth. Stir over a low heat until the sauce bubbles and thickens. Pour the sauce over the vegetables. Sprinkle the top of the casserole with cheese. Bake in a preheated 350°F oven 45 minutes or until brown and bubbly.

SERVES 4.

Travel through France's Champagne Province and you will not only be visiting the birthplace of one of the world's most glorious wines. On a drive through the flat countryside, you will see vast plantings of potatoes, which, along with beets and grain, make up much of France's food.

In the French household, the potato is thought of as an entrée or course in its own right, not merely an accompaniment to meat, fish, or fowl. French housewives and restaurant chefs, for that matter, often serve potatoes as a separate course, whipped into creamy peaks, sprinkled with cheese, or browned in the oven. Such dishes often make the main course for a luncheon or light supper.

Some of the most imaginative potato dishes—such as Pommes de Terres Anna, which consists of layers of thin potato slices cooked in butter in a hot oven until crisp and brown—was created in the northern provinces.

It was a French chef, incidentally, who came up with the crisp, puffy Soufflé Potatoes. He created it by mistake, so the story goes, when he refried some potatoes for a royal feast.

Snow Potatoes Grand Marnier

Water
2 pounds medium-sized potatoes, peeled
   and quartered
2 teaspoons salt
3 medium-sized oranges

ORANGE CREAM

1 cup dairy sour cream
   Pulp from the 3 oranges, diced
1 orange rind, grated
1 ounce Grand Marnier
1 tablespoon sugar
¼ teaspoon salt

In a large saucepan in 1 inch of water, cook the potatoes with the salt 15 to 20 minutes, until tender. Cut the oranges in half. With a sharp knife, scoop out the orange pulp in large pieces and cut into small chunks to use in the Orange Cream. Reserve the orange shells. When the potatoes are done, rice them and spoon lightly into the orange shells in high mounds. Place the shells in a large baking pan and keep warm in a 200°F oven until serving time.

Combine all Orange Cream ingredients, chill, and spoon on top of the Snow Potato filling in the orange shells. Pass remaining Orange Cream for those desiring more.

SERVES 6.

Pommes de Terre Saladaise

1½ pounds potatoes, peeled and sliced
¼ cup goose fat
½ cup green pepper, finely diced
¼ cup chopped shallots
½ pound fresh black truffles, thinly sliced
    Salt and pepper to taste
¼ teaspoon cayenne

Place the potato slices on paper towels. In a heavy skillet, heat the goose fat until foam subsides. Add the potatoes and cook over a fairly high heat, turning until light brown on all sides. Blend in the green pepper and shallots and simmer several minutes. Add the sliced truffles, using extra goose fat if needed. Continue to cook until the potatoes and green pepper are tender. Season the mixture with salt, pepper, and cayenne and serve.

SERVES 4 TO 6.

Gratin aux Champignons

5 medium-sized potatoes, peeled and
    thinly sliced
¼ teaspoon salt
¼ teaspoon pepper
1½ pounds fresh mushrooms, sliced
1 clove garlic
½ cup butter
½ teaspoon nutmeg
1 cup Swiss cheese, grated
1 small bunch parsley, chopped
1 small onion, minced
2 cups heavy cream
1 ounce Cognac

Dry the potatoes and sprinkle with salt and pepper.
Dry the mushrooms. Rub a 2-quart baking dish with garlic
and grease it with 1 tablespoon of the butter. Put in alternate layers of potatoes and mushrooms. Sprinkle each
layer with nutmeg, cheese, parsley, and onion. Finish
with a layer of potatoes and cover it with a mixture of the
cream and Cognac. Sprinkle with cheese and dot with the
remaining butter. Bake in a preheated 375°F oven until
the potatoes are easily pierced. Serve very hot.

SERVES 6 TO 8.

Pommes Savarin

6 medium-sized potatoes, peeled and cut
    into thin, matchlike sticks
1 cup butter
2 tablespoons all-purpose flour
2 tablespoons butter
1 cup milk
1 cup heavy cream
    Salt and pepper to taste
¼ teaspoon powdered mace
2 ounces cream sherry
1 tablespoon grated Romano cheese
2 teaspoons paprika

Dry the potato sticks thoroughly and put them into a 6-cup mold. Press them down and add the butter. Bake in a preheated 500°F oven about 20 minutes, until the potatoes are done and the butter is absorbed. Watch to make sure that the potatoes do not burn. Turn the brown, crusted potatoes over onto a hot serving dish and keep warm while the sauce is being made. Lightly brown the flour in 2 tablespoons butter in a saucepan over a low heat. When pasty, slowly stir in the milk and cream. Add the remaining ingredients. Cook over a low heat until thickened and spoon over the potato sticks.

SERVES 6.

12

POTATO AS A DIET FOOD

A few years ago, to prove that potatoes are not fattening per se, a Michigan State University graduate student, Robert Luescher, went on a potato diet. He ate four pounds of spuds a day in various forms: boiled for breakfast, potato salad for lunch, and fried for dinner. As all these tubers added up to only 1,300 calories a day, he deliberately added fatteners to bring his total daily intake up to 3,600 calories. Health researchers monitored Luescher, and at the end of three weeks he had put on only four ounces. Needless to say, without the addition of fatteners he undoubtedly would have lost weight.

Most Americans still believe the potato is fattening, and when they go on a diet it is the first thing they eliminate. Actually, ounce for ounce, potatoes have fewer calories than fresh peas, lima beans, or corn. A medium-sized baked potato has about the same number of calories as an eight-ounce cup of orange juice.

Those who cut out potatoes when they are trying to lose weight should bear in mind that nutritionists and physicians are opposed to fad diets that rule out whole categories of food in favor of a few limited choices. They warn that such dieting can impair your health and vitality by robbing you of the important nutrients your body needs every day. A 90-calorie baked potato will provide you with one third of the vitamin C you need daily and will also contribute vitamin B_1, niacin, and iron. In addition, the potato provides carbohydrates, which are one of the body's most important energy sources. And potatoes are great appetite appeasers.

The potato was given a bad reputation in the slim-waist set because many people drown the spud in butter, sour cream, or thick gravy. Potatoes by themselves are tasty enough for most of us, but for those who want to dress up a baked spud there are a number of tasty but low-calories toppings. Here are a few:

- Melted margarine thinned with lemon juice
- Grated Parmesan cheese in moderate amounts
- Heated skim milk or chicken broth mixed with tangy herbs
- Mock sour cream made from whipped cottage cheese and lemon juice
- Sliced mushrooms marinated in a low-calorie dressing
- A spoonful of tomatoes and coarsely grated cheese
- Whipped margarine and a dash of poppy seeds
- Chicken bouillon with minced onion and parsley
- Yogurt or cottage cheese with chives
- Chopped onion with coarsely ground pepper

Potatoes cost only pennies per pound, even at today's high food prices. But there was a time when they were worth their weight in gold. During the Gold Rush of 1898, when scurvy was striking down scores of prospectors, potatoes could be exchanged for gold on a weight-for-weight basis because the tuber's high vitamin C content helped cure or at least ward off scurvy.

Manhattan Clam Chowder

3 cans (7 ounces each) minced clams
3 medium-sized potatoes, peeled and
    diced
3 medium-sized carrots, scraped and
    sliced
4 medium-sized celery stalks, chopped
1 can (16 ounces) tomatoes
  Dash oregano
¼ teaspoon Worcestershire sauce
2 teaspoons salt
½ teaspoon thyme leaves
1 tablespoon bacon bits

In a large kettle, combine all the ingredients. Cover and simmer 1 hour.

SERVES 8, ABOUT 100 CALORIES PER SERVING.

Garden Soup

1 medium-sized onion, chopped
1 tablespoon diet margarine
3 medium-sized potatoes, peeled and
    diced
1 cup fresh green beans, diced
1 medium-sized celery stalk, sliced
2 tablespoons chopped parsley
5 cups chicken bouillon
  Dash garlic powder
  Dash cayenne

In a large nonstick kettle, cook the onion in the margarine. Add the remaining ingredients. Cover and simmer 40 minutes, until the vegetables are tender.

SERVES 8, ABOUT 55 CALORIES PER SERVING.

Diet Vichyssoise

    3 cups potatoes, peeled and cubed
 1½ cups minced onion
    4 chicken bouillon cubes
      Dash Tabasco sauce
      Dash paprika
    2 cups water
    1 cup evaporated skim milk
    1 teaspoon sherry
    2 tablespoons chopped chives

In a covered kettle, cook the potatoes, onion, bouillon cubes, Tabasco sauce, and paprika in the water 30 minutes, until the potatoes are tender. Purée the potatoes and liquid in a blender. Stir in the milk and sherry. Chill and serve topped with chives.

SERVES 6, ABOUT 120 CALORIES PER SERVING.

Legend has it that the potato had to cross the Atlantic Ocean seven times as ballast in ships before it was accepted in the American colonies. Although it occasionally found its way to settlers' tables as an imported oddity, it was not until 1719 that potatoes were cultivated in America. That happened when a group of Irish—who else?—founded the community of Londonderry in New Hampshire and began growing spuds.

Garden Meatball Soup

2 medium-sized potatoes, peeled and
    cubed
2 medium-sized carrots, peeled and
    sliced
1 medium-sized onion, chopped
4 medium-sized celery stalks with leaves,
    coarsely chopped
1 can (16 ounces) tomatoes
1 cup green beans, diced
  Dash Italian seasoning
1 teaspoon Worcestershire sauce
2 teaspoons salt
3 cups water
1 pound lean beef round, ground
1 egg, beaten
½ teaspoon garlic salt
¼ cup chopped parsley

In a large kettle, combine the potatoes, carrots, onion, celery, tomatoes, green beans, Italian seasoning, Worcestershire sauce, and salt. Add the water and simmer 30 minutes. Meanwhile, combine the ground beef, egg, garlic salt, and parsley. Shape into 1-inch balls. Add to the soup and simmer, covered, 20 minutes longer, until the meatballs are tender. This dish is a meal in itself.

SERVES 4, ABOUT 300 CALORIES PER SERVING.

Mushroom Potato Soup

½ pound fresh mushrooms, cleaned and
    chopped
1 small onion, minced
1 tablespoon diet margarine
3 tablespoons flour
5 cups water
2 medium-sized potatoes, peeled and
    cubed
¼ teaspoon Tabasco sauce
1 tablespoon lime juice
2 ounces sherry
2 teaspoons salt
  Dash paprika
  Chopped chives

In a large, heavy, nonstick kettle, cook the mushrooms and onion in margarine 5 minutes. Stir in the flour and cook 2 minutes more. Gradually add the water. Cook, stirring constantly, until the mixture thickens and boils. Add the remaining ingredients except the chives. Cover and simmer 45 minutes, until the potatoes are tender. Garnish with chives.

SERVES 8, ABOUT 55 CALORIES PER SERVING.

Alpine Potato Casserole

4 cups cooked potatoes, peeled and
    cubed
1 cup plain yogurt
1 cup low-fat cottage cheese
    Dash Tabasco sauce
¼ cup chopped chives
1 teaspoon salt
    Dash garlic powder
    Dash paprika

In a nonstick, 9-inch square baking pan, combine all the ingredients. Bake in a preheated 350°F oven 30 minutes, until hot and bubbling.

SERVES 8, ABOUT 105 CALORIES PER SERVING.

Slimdown Potato Scallop

2 cups potatoes, peeled and thinly sliced
½ cup mushrooms, sliced
½ cup onion, sliced
4 bouillon cubes
1 ounce Scotch
1½ cups boiling water
1 teaspoon salt
¼ teaspoon thyme leaves
    Dash cayenne

In a nonstick 9-inch-square baking pan, combine the potatoes, mushrooms, and onion. Place the bouillon cubes and Scotch in the boiling water. Add the salt, thyme, and cayenne. Pour over the vegetables. Cover and bake in a preheated 350°F oven 30 minutes. Uncover and bake 15 more minutes, until the vegetables are tender.

SERVES 6, ABOUT 55 CALORIES PER SERVING.

Potato-Paprika Hash

1 medium-sized onion, sliced
1 tablespoon peanut oil
1 cup potatoes, boiled, peeled, and
  cubed
2 medium-sized celery stalks, sliced
1 package (10 ounces) frozen mixed
  vegetables
1 teaspoon salt
½ teaspoon paprika
  Dash Tabasco sauce
1 can condensed beef bouillon
1 tablespoon cornstarch
⅓ cup cold water

In a medium-sized heavy, nonstick skillet, cook the onion in the oil 5 minutes, stirring occasionally. Add the potatoes and celery and cook 5 minutes more. Stir in the mixed vegetables, salt, paprika, and Tabasco sauce. Add the bouillon. Cover and cook 20 minutes, stirring occasionally and separating the frozen vegetables. In a cup, mix the cornstarch with the cold water. Gradually add to the vegetable mixture. Cook, stirring constantly, until the hash thickens.

SERVES 6, ABOUT 85 CALORIES PER SERVING.

Potato Tomato Pot

2 medium-sized potatoes, peeled and
　　diced
1 medium-sized tomato, cut up
1 medium-sized onion, sliced
　Dash Tabasco sauce
¾ teaspoon salt
　Dash paprika
1 tablespoon peanut oil

In a small baking dish, toss all the ingredients together. Cover and bake in a preheated 350°F oven 30 minutes. Uncover and bake 30 minutes more, until the potatoes are tender.

SERVES 4, ABOUT 90 CALORIES PER SERVING.

Pommes au Gratin

3 medium-sized potatoes, peeled,
　　cooked, and sliced
½ cup chopped onions
½ cup coarsely chopped celery
1 can (10¾ ounces) condensed cheddar
　　cheese soup
1 tablespoon prepared mustard
　Dash Worcestershire sauce

In a nonstick 9-inch-square baking pan, combine the potatoes, onions, and celery. Blend the soup, mustard, and Worcestershire sauce and pour over the vegetables. Bake in a preheated 375°F oven 30 minutes, until hot.

SERVES 8, ABOUT 80 CALORIES PER SERVING.

Potato-Cheese Casserole

3 medium-sized potatoes, cooked, peeled
   and mashed with skim milk
1 package (3½ to 4 ounces) Neufchatel
   cheese
1 egg, lightly beaten
  Dash Tabasco sauce
2 tablespoons chopped chives
1 tablespoon chopped parsley
  Salt and pepper to taste
  Cayenne to taste

Combine the mashed potatoes and cheese, beating until well blended. Stir in the egg, Tabasco sauce, chives, and parsley. Add the salt and pepper, mix, and spoon into a well-greased 1-quart casserole. Sprinkle with cayenne. Bake in a preheated 400°F oven 30 minutes, until heated through.

SERVES 8, ABOUT 80 CALORIES PER SERVING.

Potatoes Cottage Style

4 medium-sized potatoes, baked
1 cup low-fat cottage cheese
½ cup buttermilk
1 tablespoon minced onion
½ teaspoon salt
Dash rosemary
Paprika
2 tablespoons chopped parsley

Cut hot potatoes in half lengthwise. Scoop out the pulp, leaving the shells intact. Whip the potatoes with remaining ingredients except the paprika and parsley. Pile the mixture into the shells. Sprinkle with paprika and parsley. Bake in a preheated 400°F oven 10 minutes, until golden.

SERVES 8, ABOUT 75 CALORIES PER SERVING.

Baked Potato Strips

4 medium-sized potatoes, peeled and cut
    into strips
2 tablespoons peanut oil
Salt and cayenne to taste

Put the potato strips, after cutting each one, into a bowl of ice water to crisp. Drain and pat dry with paper towels. Spread the strips in a jelly-roll pan. Sprinkle with oil. Shake the pan to distribute the oil evenly over the potatoes. Bake the strips in a preheated 450°F oven 30 to 45 minutes, turning often. Sprinkle with salt and cayenne.

SERVES 8, ABOUT 100 CALORIES PER SERVING.

Potatoes and Green Beans

    3 medium-sized potatoes, peeled and
        cubed
    1 teaspoon salt
    ⅛ teaspoon garlic powder
    ¼ teaspoon Italian seasoning
        Water
    1 package (9 ounces) frozen French-style
        green beans
    2 teaspoons cornstarch

Cook the potatoes with salt, garlic powder, and Italian seasoning in 1 inch of water 15 minutes. Add the green beans and cook 10 minutes more, until the vegetables are tender. Drain, reserving ¾ cup of the cooking liquid. In a cup, blend the cornstarch with 1 tablespoon cold water and then stir into the reserved cooking liquid. Cook, stirring, until thickened, about 2 minutes. Add the vegetables and reheat.

SERVES 4, ABOUT 85 CALORIES PER SERVING.

Pepper-Potato Casserole

4 medium-sized potatoes, peeled and
   sliced
1 medium-sized onion, peeled and sliced
3 medium-sized green peppers, diced
1 can (10¾ ounces) condensed cream of
   potato soup
Dash salt, pepper, and Tabasco sauce

In a nonstick 8-inch-square baking pan, alternately
layer the potatoes, onion, and peppers. Combine the
soup with the seasonings, add 1 soup can of water, and
pour over the vegetables. Bake, covered, in a preheated
350°F oven 30 minutes. Uncover and bake 30 minutes
longer, until the vegetables are tender.

SERVES 6, ABOUT 110 CALORIES PER SERVING.

Bouillon Potatoes

Water
6 medium-sized potatoes, peeled and
   thinly sliced
½ cup minced shallots
1 clove garlic, minced
1 cup condensed beef bouillon
½ cup chopped parsley
   Salt, pepper, and paprika to taste

In a large saucepan, in 1 inch of water, combine the
potatoes, shallots, garlic, and bouillon. Cover and cook 15
minutes. Add the parsley and cook 5 minutes longer.
Drain and sprinkle with salt, pepper, and paprika.

SERVES 6, ABOUT 90 CALORIES PER SERVING.

Ragout of Beef

2 pounds lean, well-trimmed beef round
    steak, cubed
¾ cup chopped onion
¾ cup diced green peppers
  Vegetable oil
2 cups water
1 can (16 ounces) tomatoes
½ cup dry red wine
¼ teaspoon Tabasco sauce
2 beef bouillon cubes
2 tablespoons flour
2 teaspoons salt
1 teaspoon paprika
  Dash pepper
  Dash garlic powder
4 medium-sized potatoes, peeled and
    cubed
1 cup chopped celery

In a large, heavy, nonstick Dutch oven, brown the meat, onion, and peppers in oil. Drain off any accumulated fat. Add the water and the remaining ingredients except the potatoes and celery. Cover and simmer 1 hour, until the meat is almost tender. Add the potatoes and celery. Cook another 30 minutes, until the meat and vegetables are tender.

SERVES 8, ABOUT 300 CALORIES PER SERVING.

Beef and Potato Moussaka

1 pound lean ground beef round
½ cup green pepper, diced
1 medium-sized onion, chopped
2 medium-sized potatoes, peeled and
　　sliced
1 can (8 ounces) tomato sauce
　Dash Tabasco sauce
1 teaspoon salt
　Dash pepper
　Dash garlic powder
2 eggs
1 cup plain yogurt

In a large, heavy, nonstick skillet with an oven-proof handle, brown the meat, green pepper, and onion. Drain off any accumulated fat. Add the potatoes, tomato sauce, Tabasco sauce, salt, pepper, and garlic powder. Cook five minutes, stirring constantly. Spread the mixture evenly at the bottom of the skillet. In a medium-sized bowl, beat the eggs lightly with a fork, blend in the yogurt, and spread over the meat mixture. Bake in a preheated 350°F oven 1 hour, until the topping is set. Let stand 10 minutes before serving.

SERVES 4, ABOUT 320 CALORIES PER SERVING.

Frankfurter Scallop

4 medium-sized potatoes, peeled and
　　thinly sliced
1 medium-sized onion, peeled and thinly
　　sliced
8 frankfurters, cut into 1-inch chunks
2 ounces dry white wine
1½ cups skim milk

4 teaspoons flour
1 teaspoon salt
  Dash cayenne
1 tablespoon prepared mustard

In a nonstick 9-inch-square baking pan, layer half of the potatoes followed by layers of the onion, frankfurters, and remaining potatoes. In a small bowl, combine the wine, milk, flour, salt, cayenne, and mustard. Pour over the casserole. Bake in a preheated 375°F oven 1 hour, until hot and bubbling

SERVES 6, ABOUT 280 CALORIES PER SERVING.

Slim-Down Corned Beef and Cabbage

4 pounds corned beef round (less
    fattening than brisket)
3 bay leaves
  Water
4 medium-sized potatoes, peeled and
    quartered
3 large carrots, scraped and sliced
1 large head cabbage, cut into wedges

In a heavy Dutch oven, place the corned beef and bay leaves. Add enough water to cover. Heat the water to a boil and skim the surface. Cover and simmer over a low heat about 4 hours or until meat is nearly tender. Remove the cover and skim off surface fat. Add the potatoes and carrots and cook another 20 minutes. Add the cabbage and simmer until the meat and vegetables are tender, about 10 minutes. One serving consists of ¼ pound corned beef, ½ potato, ½ cup cabbage, and a couple of carrot slices. The leftover corned beef is good cold.

SERVES 8, ABOUT 310 CALORIES PER SERVING.

Potato-Crust Ham and Cheese

2 cups potatoes, peeled, cooked, and
    mashed with skim milk
2 tablespoons prepared mustard
½ teaspoon Worcestershire sauce
¼ teaspoon pepper
1 pound boiled ham, cubed
½ cup low-fat cottage cheese
2 slices low-fat cheddar cheese,
    crumbled

Mix the mashed potatoes and mustard with the Worcestershire sauce and pepper. Spread evenly in the bottom of a nonstick 8-inch-square baking pan. Add the ham cubes in a layer on top of the potatoes. In a blender, blend the cottage cheese and cheddar cheese until fairly smooth. Spread over the ham. Bake in a preheated 350°F oven 30 minutes, until the casserole is heated through.

SERVES 5, ABOUT 250 CALORIES PER SERVING.

Italian Veal Stew

8 pieces veal shank (2 to 3 pounds), well
    trimmed
1 tablespoon peanut oil
1 medium-sized onion, diced
1 clove garlic, minced
½ cup rosé wine
1 teaspoon Worcestershire sauce
1 tablespoon lime juice
2 cups chicken broth
1 teaspoon Italian seasoning
4 medium-sized potatoes, peeled and
    quartered
4 medium-sized carrots, peeled and
    chopped

2 medium-sized celery stalks, chopped
1 tablespoon chopped parsley

In a large, heavy, nonstick Dutch oven, brown the veal in the oil. Add the onion and garlic and cook 5 minutes. Stir in the wine, Worcestershire sauce, lime juice, chicken broth, and Italian seasoning. Cover and simmer 1 hour, until the meat is almost tender. Add the remaining ingredients, and simmer, covered, another 30 minutes, until the meat and vegetables are tender.

SERVES 8, ABOUT 235 CALORIES PER SERVING.

Danish Pork Chops

6 center-cut pork chops, well trimmed
2 medium-sized potatoes, peeled and
   quartered
2 cups chicken broth
1 teaspoon salt
½ teaspoon nutmeg
   Dash Tabasco sauce
1 teaspoon curry powder
   Dash paprika
1 coarsely chopped apple
1 tablespoon lime juice
   Liquid sugar substitute, *optional*

In a large, heavy, nonstick skillet, brown the chops on both sides, draining off any accumulated fat. Add the potatoes, chicken broth, salt, nutmeg, Tabasco sauce, curry powder, and paprika. Cover and simmer 45 minutes, until the pork chops are almost tender. Add the apple and lime juice and simmer 15 minutes more. Just before serving, stir in a few drops of sugar substitute, if desired.

SERVES 6, ABOUT 290 CALORIES PER SERVING.

Dilled Lamb Stew

1½ pounds lean, trimmed lamb, cubed
10 small onions, peeled
 1 cup water
¾ cup tomato juice
   Dash Tabasco sauce
½ teaspoon Worcestershire sauce
 2 teaspoons dill weed
 2 teaspoons salt
   Dash pepper
 5 medium-sized potatoes, peeled and
     cut into chunks
 5 medium-sized carrots, peeled and
     diced
 1 package (10 ounces) frozen peas

In a large, heavy, a nonstick Dutch oven, brown the lamb and onions. Drain off any accumulated fat. Stir in the water, tomato juice, Tabasco sauce, Worcestershire sauce, dill, salt, and pepper. Cover and simmer 1 hour, until the lamb is almost tender. Add the potatoes and carrots. Cook, covered, 30 minutes longer. Add the peas and cook 10 minutes or until the meat and vegetables are tender.

SERVES 10, ABOUT 300 CALORIES PER SERVING.

Ground Lamb Ring with Potato Puffs

2 pounds lean ground lamb
3 eggs
  Dash Tabasco sauce
½ cup chopped green pepper
2 tablespoons minced onion
1 tablespoon chopped parsley
1 teaspoon salt
  Dash cayenne
3 cups potatoes, peeled, cooked, and
    mashed with skim milk

In a large bowl, combine the lamb, 2 of the eggs, the Tabasco sauce, green pepper, onion, parsley, salt, and cayenne. Press the mixture into an 8-inch ring mold. Bake in a preheated 350°F oven 1 hour. Spoon off any accumulated fat. Unmold onto a large, shallow, nonstick baking pan. Beat the remaining egg into the mashed potatoes. Spoon the potatoes into individual mounds around the lamb ring. Bake in a preheated 425°F oven 10 minutes or until the potatoes are lightly browned.

SERVES 8, ABOUT 225 CALORIES PER SERVING.

Baked Italian Chicken and Potatoes

1 chicken broiler-fryer (about 3 pounds),
    cut up
2 medium-sized potatoes, peeled and
    diced
1 small onion, sliced
1 cup tomato juice
½ teaspoon Worcestershire sauce
1 teaspoon salt
½ teaspoon Italian seasoning
    Dash cayenne
    Dash garlic powder

In a large nonstick baking pan, bake the chicken pieces skin side up in a preheated 350°F oven 30 minutes, until golden brown. Baste occasionally with pan juices. Drain off accumulated fat and add the remaining ingredients. Cover and bake 30 minutes longer, until the chicken and vegetables are tender. Baste with pan juices frequently during cooking.

SERVES 6, ABOUT 235 CALORIES PER SERVING.

Country Chicken Stew

1 chicken broiler-fryer (about 3 pounds),
    cut up
1½ cups water
1 can (10¾ ounces) condensed cream of
    chicken soup
2 ounces dry white wine
3 medium-sized celery stalks, cut up
1 medium-sized onion, quartered

1 teaspoon salt
1 teaspoon poultry seasoning
3 medium-sized potatoes, peeled and
    quartered
4 medium-sized carrots, scraped and cut
    into large chunks

Under the broiler, brown the chicken pieces, skin side up. Drain off fat. In a large Dutch oven, place the chicken and the remaining ingredients except the potatoes and carrots. Cover and cook 30 minutes. Skim off fat. Add potatoes and carrots and cook 30 minutes more, until the chicken and vegetables are tender.

SERVES 6, ABOUT 310 CALORIES PER SERVING.

Turkey and Potato Bake

2 medium-sized potatoes, peeled and
    thinly sliced
2 cups cooked turkey breast, diced
1 medium-sized onion, sliced
1 can (10¾ ounces) condensed cream of
    celery soup
½ cup skim milk
¼ teaspoon poultry seasoning
   Dash cayenne

In a nonstick 8-inch-square baking pan, arrange the potatoes, turkey, and onion in alternating layers. In a small bowl, blend the soup, milk, poultry seasoning, and cayenne. Pour over the casserole. Cover and bake in a preheated 375°F oven 45 minutes. Uncover and bake 15 minutes longer or until the potatoes are tender.

SERVES 4, ABOUT 250 CALORIES PER SERVING.

Diet Salmon Loaf

2 cans (7¾ ounces each) salmon, drained
2 eggs
  Dash Tabasco sauce
1 cup potatoes, peeled, cooked, and
    mashed with skim milk
1 tablespoon minced onion
1 tablespoon chopped parsley
½ teaspoon salt
  Dash cayenne

In a medium-sized bowl, mix with a fork all the ingredients until well blended. Spread in a nonstick loaf pan. Bake in a preheated 375°F oven 40 minutes.

SERVES 5, ABOUT 180 CALORIES PER SERVING.

Chicken-Potato Curry

2 cups potatoes, peeled and thinly sliced
2 hard-cooked eggs, sliced
2 cups chicken breasts, boned and cubed
1 can (10¾ ounces) condensed cream of
    celery soup
  Dash paprika
1 tablespoon curry powder
½ cup water

In a nonstick 9-inch-square baking pan, arrange in alternate layers 1 cup of the potatoes, the eggs, the chicken, and the remaining potatoes. In a small bowl, blend the soup, paprika, curry powder, and water. Pour over the casserole. Bake in a preheated 375°F oven 1 hour, until the potatoes are tender.

SERVES 5, ABOUT 360 CALORIES PER SERVING.

Trim Tuna Hash

1 tablespoon diet margarine
2 cans (6½ to 7 ounces each)
    water-packed tuna
2 cups potatoes, cooked, peeled, and
    diced
½ cup chopped onion
½ cup chopped green pepper
3 tablespoons chopped pimiento
1 can (7¾ ounces) chicken gravy

In a medium-sized nonstick skillet, heat the margarine. Meanwhile, in a medium-sized bowl, combine the remaining ingredients. Spread the tuna mixture in the skillet and cook 15 minutes, until browned on one side. Turn over and cook 15 minutes, until heated through and browned on the other side.

SERVES 4, ABOUT 240 CALORIES PER SERVING.

13

THE FROZEN POTATO

With potatoes growing in popularity all over the world, it was inevitable that someone would come up with a simple, timesaving way for single persons or working wives to fix them. Now, owing to the development of practical methods of quick freezing, it is possible to serve all sorts of tasty potato dishes that have all the nutrients and flavor of freshly harvested spuds.

The most popular type, of course, is french fries, either popped in the oven for about 20 minutes or crisped in a greased skillet in about a third that time. But french fries have other uses. Today people are trying them in soups, casseroles, and even salads.

The french fry is not the only frozen potato product on the market. Hashed browns, either southern-style or shredded, are gaining in popularity, and so are the tasty little pellets known as potato rounds. Also available at a somewhat higher cost are packages containing delicious scalloped potatoes, potatoes au gratin, and stuffed baked spuds.

Statistics show that today more than 25 percent of all potatoes consumed in the United States are frozen. This explains why food stores have allocated 100 percent more freezer space to frozen potato products since 1960.

Canadian Soup

1 cup hot water
2 chicken bouillon cubes
1 package (9 ounces) frozen french fries
2 teaspoons instant minced onion
3 cups milk
1 can (10½ ounces) condensed cream of
    celery soup
⅛ teaspoon paprika
⅛ teaspoon pepper
1 package (8 ounces) American cheese,
    shredded
Chopped chives, *optional*

Combine the water, bouillon cubes, and french fries in a saucepan. Cook over a moderate heat about 5 minutes, or until the potatoes are mushy. Beat until smooth with a rotary or electric beater. Add the remaining ingredients except the cheese and chives, and heat. Add the cheese and stir until melted. Serve hot, plain, or garnished with added shredded cheese and chopped chives.

SERVES 4 TO 5.

French Fry Curry Soup

　1 package (9 ounces) frozen french
　　　fries, broken into bits
　1 cup diced celery
　2 chicken bouillon cubes
　½ cup water
　2 tablespoons flour
　½ teaspoon salt
　1 teaspoon curry powder
　2 cups milk
　3 tablespoons butter

Combine the french fries, celery, bouillon cubes, and water in a saucepan. Cover, bring to a boil, and simmer 5 minutes. Uncover. In a bowl, blend the flour, salt, and curry powder. Stir in the milk gradually and beat until smooth. Add to the vegetables gradually, stirring all the time. Add the butter. Cook over a low heat, stirring constantly, until slightly thickened.

SERVES 4.

French Fry Shrimp Bisque

　1 package (9 ounces) frozen french fries,
　　　broken into small pieces
　½ cup water
　2½ cups milk
　1 can (4½ ounces) deveined shrimp,
　　　drained and cut into small bits
　½ teaspoon salt
　¼ teaspoon onion salt
　1 tablespoon finely chopped parsley
　1 cup processed American cheese,
　　　shredded

Combine the potatoes and water in a saucepan and cover. Simmer about 5 minutes, until the french fries heat. Add the remaining ingredients and heat slowly until the cheese melts, stirring often. Serve piping hot.

SERVES 4.

Quick-Made Tuna Casserole

2 cans (10½ ounces each) condensed
    cream of mushroom soup
¼ cup milk
½ teaspoon salt
2 tablespoons chopped pimientos
1 cup cooked celery, diced
2 packages (9 ounces each) frozen french
    fries
1 can (7 ounces) flaked tuna, packed in oil

Combine the soup, milk, and salt in a saucepan and stir until smooth. Place over a low heat and simmer, stirring often. Add the pimientos and celery and mix. Spread half of the french fries in the bottom of a shallow 1½-quart casserole. Pour half of the hot sauce over the potatoes and cover with the flaked tuna. Top with the remaining potatoes and cover with the sauce. Heat in a preheated 400°F oven 10 minutes. Remove from the oven, mix slightly, and bake another 10 minutes, until heated through.

SERVES 6.

Beef and French Fry Meat Loaf

1½ pounds ground beef chuck
½ cup quick-cooking oats
2 eggs, slightly beaten
⅓ cup chopped onions
½ cup catsup or chili sauce
2 teaspoons salt
⅛ teaspoon pepper
1 package (9 ounces) frozen french fries
Prepared cheese spread or homemade
cheese sauce, *optional*

Mix together all the ingredients except the french fries and cheese spread or sauce. Divide the mixture into 3 equal portions. Layer one portion in the bottom of a greased loaf pan (9- by 5- by 3-inches). Press half of the french fries into the layer of the meat mixture. Cover with a second layer of the meat mixture, followed by the remaining potatoes. Pack the rest of the meat mixture on top, forming a compact loaf. Bake in a preheated 350°F oven about 1 hour, until done. Let stand 10 minutes before removing from the pan. Serve plain or with spread (melted) cheese or sauce.

SERVES 6 TO 8.

Thomas Jefferson is credited with introducing the french fry to Americans when he served it to dinner guests at the White House. John Adams thought Tom was putting on airs by serving "such novelties."

One Dish Turkey Dinner

¼ cup butter
¼ cup flour
1 teaspoon salt
Dash pepper
2½ cups milk
1 can (4 ounces) mushroom pieces and
stems, drained
¼ cup diced pimientos
1 package (10 ounces) frozen mixed
vegetables
1 package (1 pound) frozen french fries
1⅓ cups or 2 cans (5½ ounces) cooked,
boned turkey pieces

Melt the butter in a saucepan over a low heat. Blend in the flour and salt and pepper and remove from heat. Stir in the milk. Cook over a low heat, stirring, until the mixture is smooth and thick. Fold in the remaining ingredients. Pour into a 2-quart baking dish and place in a preheated 400°F oven. Stir gently after 10 minutes to speed heating. Continue baking another 10 minutes before serving.

SERVES 4.

Quick Salmon Dinner

1 can (10½ ounces) condensed cream of
celery soup
½ cup milk
½ teaspoon celery salt
¼ teaspoon salt
Dash pepper
1 can (4 ounces) mushroom pieces and
stems, drained
1 package (10 ounces) frozen green peas
1 package (1 pound) frozen french fries
1 can (1 pound) salmon, drained, boned,
and flaked

In a saucepan, combine the soup, milk, and seasonings and heat. Stir in the mushrooms and peas. Spread
half of the french fries and salmon in the bottom of a
2-quart baking dish. Cover with half of the sauce. Top
with the remaining potatoes and salmon, followed by the
rest of the sauce. Place in a preheated 400°F oven 20
minutes, until heated through.

SERVES 4.

French Fry Meat Bake

¼ cup butter
¼ cup flour
1½ teaspoons salt
½ teaspoon celery salt
¼ teaspoon onion salt
Dash pepper
2½ cups milk
¼ cup prepared mustard
1 package (1 pound) frozen french fries

1 package (10 ounces) frozen green
   beans
1 can (12 ounces) luncheon meat, sliced

Melt the butter in a saucepan and stir in the flour and seasonings except the mustard. Remove from heat and stir in the milk. Return to heat. Cook, stirring, until smooth and thick. Stir in the mustard. Fold the french fries, green beans, and luncheon meat into the sauce. Pour into a 2-quart baking dish. Heat in a preheated 400°F oven about 20 minutes.

SERVES 4.

Bacon French Fry Casserole

1 pound bacon cut into ½-inch bits
⅓ cup bacon drippings
⅓ cup flour
¼ teaspoon pepper
½ teaspoon dried parsley flakes
½ cup chopped onion
3 cups milk
1 cup canned tomatoes
1 package (1 pound) frozen french fries
1 package (10 ounces) frozen peas and
   carrots

Fry the bacon bits slowly until crisp, stirring to brown evenly. Drain and save the drippings. In a saucepan, combine the drippings, flour, pepper, parsley, and onion. Gradually add the milk. Cook, stirring, until smooth and thickened. Fold in the bacon bits and the remaining ingredients. Pour into a 2-quart baking dish. Bake in a preheated 400°F oven about 20 minutes, until heated, stirring gently at the end of 10 minutes to speed heating.

SERVES 6.

Fish Potato Roll-Ups

1 pound flounder or sole fillets
1 tablespoon dried parsley flakes
1½ teaspoons salt
¼ teaspoon coarsely ground pepper
1 package (9 ounces) frozen french fries
2 tablespoons butter
1 can (8 ounces) tomato sauce

Separate or cut the fish fillets into six portions. Sprinkle with parsley, salt, and pepper. Roll the fish around the french fries, making six bundles. Melt the butter in a small baking dish. Place the bundles with the potatoes upright in the baking dish and pour the tomato sauce over them. Bake in a preheated 350°F oven 25 minutes.

SERVES 4.

Crab Meat French Fry Supreme

¼ cup chopped onion
2 tablespoons butter
1 can (10½ ounces) condensed cream of
    celery soup
1 cup processed American cheese,
    shredded
1 egg, slightly beaten
1 package (6 ounces) frozen crab meat,
    flaked and thawed
¼ cup milk
½ teaspoon paprika
2 tablespoons dry sherry
1 tablespoon parsley, finely chopped
2 packages (1 pound each) frozen french
    fries

In a pan, sauté the onion in the butter until soft but not brown. Stir in the soup, cheese, egg, crab meat, milk, and paprika. Heat slowly until almost boiling, stirring occasionally. Add the sherry and parsley just before serving. Brown the french fries in the oven, broiler, or frying pan and serve the crab meat mixture over them.

SERVES 4 TO 6.

Potatoes Italiano

    1 pound sweet Italian sausage, cut into
        small pieces
    1 medium-sized onion, thinly sliced
    1 can (1 pound 12 ounces) Italian-style
        tomatoes
    1 teaspoon salt
    1 teaspoon oregano
    ¼ teaspoon basil
    ⅛ teaspoon pepper
    2 packages (9 ounces each) frozen french
        fries
    1 package (8 ounces) mozzarella cheese,
        cut into strips
    ¼ cup grated Parmesan cheese
    1 teaspoon dried parsley flakes

Cook the sausage slowly over a moderate heat until lightly browned, stirring as needed to brown evenly. Add the onion and cook until soft. Add the tomatoes, salt, oregano, basil, and pepper and heat. Spread 1 package of the frozen french fries in the bottom of a 2-quart casserole. Cover with the mozzarella cheese and the tomato mixture. Top with the remaining french fries. Sprinkle Parmesan cheese and parsley flakes over the potatoes. Bake in a preheated 350°F oven 45 minutes, until thoroughly heated.

SERVES 4 TO 6.

French Fry Cheese Broil

1 package (9 ounces) frozen french fries
⅓ cup commercial Italian dressing
1 teaspoon chopped fresh onion
1 tablespoon chopped fresh parsley
1 cup processed American cheese,
    shredded

Empty the french fries into a shallow aluminum foil pan. Brush the potatoes with the Italian dressing. Sprinkle with onion and parsley. Place in the broiler at a moderate temperature, 4 to 6 inches from the heat. Heat and brown about 8 to 12 minutes. Sprinkle the cheese over the potatoes and broil until the cheese softens.

SERVES 2.

Fries and Chicken Pie

    2 packages (9 ounces each) frozen french
        fries
    4 eggs, slightly beaten
    1 cup milk
 1½ cups cooked chicken, boned and diced
    1 package (10 ounces) frozen green peas,
        thawed
    1 tablespoon chopped onion
    1 teaspoon minced fresh parsley
    2 tablespoons chopped pimientos
    2 teaspoons salt
    1 teaspoon tarragon
   ¼ teaspoon pepper
    1 can (10½ ounces) cream of mushroom
        soup

Line the bottom and sides of a buttered 9-inch pie pan with ⅔ of the french fries, standing the potatoes up on end around the edge of the pan. Mix together the eggs, ⅓ cup of the milk, the chicken, peas, onion, parsley, pimientos, salt, tarragon, and pepper. Pour the mixture over the potatoes. Arrange the remaining potatoes on top of the pie pan. Bake in a preheated 375°F oven about 45 minutes, until the mixture is set. Combine the mushroom soup and the remaining milk and heat. Serve as a sauce with the pie.

SERVES 6.

French Spareribs Bake

4 pounds spareribs, cut into 2-rib portions
1¾ teaspoons salt
½ cup tomato-based barbecue sauce
1 package (1 pound) frozen french fries
  Dash pepper
½ cup coarsely chopped onion
½ cup finely chopped celery
1 tablespoon flour
¾ cup water

Place the spareribs in a shallow baking pan. Sprinkle with 1 teaspoon of the salt. Cover with aluminum foil, crimping tightly to the edges of the pan. Bake in a preheated 400°F oven 30 minutes. Remove the foil and continue baking 40 minutes, until almost tender. Stand the ribs up on the sides of the pan, brush them with half of the barbecue sauce, and then place them flat again. Add the fries and sprinkle with ½ teaspoon of the salt and the pepper. In a skillet, combine ¼ cup of the drippings from the ribs with the onion and celery and sauté about 5 minutes, until the onion is soft but not brown. Blend in the flour and the remaining ¼ teaspoon salt. Add the water and cook until thickened, stirring water and cook until thickened, stirring constantly. Stir constantly. Stir in the remaining barbecue sauce. Pour over the ribs and fries. Return to the oven and bake at 400°F about 30 minutes, until the fries are heated and slightly browned and the ribs are tender.

SERVES 4.

Flaked French and Vegetables

CREAMED VEGETABLES

> ½ cup butter
> ¼ cup flour
> ½ teaspoon salt
>   Dash pepper
> 2 cups milk
> 1 package (10 ounces) frozen green peas
> ½ cup coarsely chopped mushrooms
> 2 tablespoons chopped pimientos

FLAKED FRENCH

> 1 egg
> ¼ teaspoon salt
> 1½ teaspoons onion salt
> 1 package (9 ounces) frozen french fries
> 1 cup crushed cornflakes
> ¼ cup cooking oil

Melt the butter in a saucepan over a low heat and stir in the flour, salt, and pepper. Blend in the milk and cook, stirring, over a low heat until thickened. Fold in the peas, mushrooms, and pimientos and heat through.

To prepare the Flaked French, combine the egg with the seasonings and beat slightly. Dip the french fries into the egg mixture. Roll each french fry in cornflakes and fry in hot oil over a moderate heat until golden brown all over. Serve the potatoes on top of the Creamed Vegetables.

SERVES 4.

Potatoes Milano

¼ cup melted butter
3 tablespoons flour
1 teaspoon salt
Dash pepper
¼ teaspoon oregano
2 cups milk
1 package (1 pound) frozen french fries
1 can (2½ to 3 ounces) grated Parmesan
   cheese

Blend together the butter, flour, salt, pepper, and oregano in a saucepan. Gradually add the milk. Cook over a low heat, stirring until smooth and thickened. Fold in the french fries and half of the Parmesan cheese. Arrange 4 servings in individual baking dishes. Bake in a preheated 400°F oven 15 minutes, until heated through. Remove from the oven and make a border of Parmesan cheese around the edge of the casseroles. Sprinkle as desired with additional oregano. Return to the oven 4 minutes more to soften the cheese slightly.

SERVES 4.

Harlequin Potatoes

⅓ cup butter
½ cup diced green pepper
⅓ cup flour
1 teaspoon salt
⅛ teaspoon pepper
3 cups milk
¼ cup diced pimientos

½ pound processed American cheese,
   shredded
1 package (1 pound) frozen french fries

Melt the butter in a skillet and sauté the green pepper until tender but not brown. Blend in the flour, salt, and pepper. Remove from heat and stir in the milk. Cook, stirring, until smooth and thickened. Fold in the pimientos, half of the cheese, and the french fries. Pour into a 2-quart baking dish and place in a preheated 400°F oven 15 minutes. Remove from the oven and sprinkle the remaining cheese around the edges of the casserole. Return to the oven to soften the cheese slightly, about 4 minutes longer.

SERVES 4 TO 6.

French Fries in Sour Cream Sauce

1 package (9 ounces) frozen french fries
3 tablespoons butter
½ teaspoon salt
1 tablespoon flour
1 pint dairy sour cream
2 tablespoons thinly sliced green onion
½ teaspoon marjoram
1 vegetable bouillon cube, finely crushed

In a skillet, brown the french fries in 1 tablespoon of the butter and sprinkle with the salt. Keep warm. Melt the remaining butter in a saucepan, and blend in the flour. Add the sour cream, green onion, marjoram, and bouillon cube. Heat, stirring constantly. Add the french fries and stir carefully to coat the potatoes evenly.

SERVES 4.

Cheese-Herb French Fries

1 package (1 pound) frozen french fries
¼ cup grated American cheese
½ teaspoon celery salt
Dash basil

Heat the french fries in the oven as directed on the package. Before serving, sprinkle with cheese, celery salt, and basil. Mix gently.

SERVES 3 TO 4.

Au Gratin Potatoes

⅓ cup butter
⅓ cup flour
1½ teaspoons salt
Dash pepper
3 cups milk
2 packages (9 ounces) frozen french fries
8 ounces grated American cheese
⅓ cup cornflakes, crushed and buttered

In a saucepan, melt the butter over a low heat and stir in the flour, salt, and pepper. Blend in the milk and cook over a low heat until thickened, stirring constantly. Spread half of the french fries in the bottom of a 2-quart flat baking dish. Cover with half of the sauce and sprinkle with half of the cheese. Repeat with the remaining potatoes, sauce, and cheese. Sprinkle the cornflakes around the edges of the dish. Bake in a preheated 400°F oven until heated through, about 20 minutes.

SERVES 4 TO 6.

Potato Pagoda

2½ pounds beef flank steak
   Salt and pepper to taste
½ cup parsley, finely chopped
   Cooking oil
1 package (1 pound 4 ounces) frozen
   shoestring potatoes
1 can Chinese vegetables, drained well
1 bunch celery hearts, sliced
1 pound fresh mushrooms, sliced
1 clove crushed garlic
1 tablespoon soy sauce
2 teaspoons sugar

Pound the flank steak flat. Sprinkle with salt, pepper, and parsley and cut into 1½-inch slices. Brown on both sides in a large heavy skillet in a little hot oil. Stir-fry the potatoes in a lightly greased skillet until browned. Keep the steak and potatoes warm in the oven. Add more oil to the skillet and stir-fry the Chinese vegetables, celery, mushrooms, and garlic. Add soy sauce and sugar. Taste to correct the seasoning, if necessary. Serve the potatoes on a platter, covered or surrounded with the meat and vegetables.

SERVES 6.

Peter Piper Pickle Stew

 2 cans (1½ pounds each) beef stew
 1 cup thinly sliced dill pickles
 ½ to ¾ pound frozen shoestring potatoes
   Salt to taste
 1 cup dairy sour cream
 1 cup finely sliced green onions

In a large saucepan, combine the stew and pickles and simmer to blend the flavors. Prepare the shoestring potatoes according to the directions on the package, and season with salt. Line the sides of a 2-quart serving dish with the potatoes, placing the remainder on the bottom. Pour the stew into the dish and pour the sour cream around the edges. Sprinkle with green onions.

SERVES 6.

Captain's Casserole

 ½ cup chopped green pepper
 ¼ cup chopped onion
 ¼ cup butter
 3 tablespoons flour
 1½ teaspoons salt
 ½ teaspoon dill weed
 ¼ teaspoon pepper
 1 can (13 ounces) evaporated milk
 1 can (3 ounces) sliced, broiled mush-
    rooms
 2 cans (6 ounces each) white tuna,
    drained and flaked
 1 package (10 ounces) frozen peas,
    partially thawed and separated
 1 tablespoon Worcestershire sauce
 1 pound frozen potato rounds

Cook the green pepper and onion in the butter until tender but not brown. Blend in the flour and seasonings. Gradually add the milk and mushroom liquid. Cook and stir until smooth and thickened. Add the tuna, peas, mushrooms, and Worcestershire sauce. Spoon the mixture into a 2-quart casserole. Place the potato rounds on top of the mixture. Bake in a preheated 375°F oven 30 minutes, until hot and bubbling.

SERVES 6.

Nugget Nests

    2 pounds ground beef
    ¾ cup soft bread crumbs
    ½ cup milk
    1 egg, beaten
    ¼ cup chopped green pepper
    1 small onion, grated
    2 teaspoons salt
    1 teaspoon Worcestershire sauce
    ½ teaspoon poultry seasoning
    ¾ cup catsup
    ¼ cup water
    1 pound frozen potato rounds

Combine the ground beef, bread crumbs, milk, egg, green pepper, onion, salt, Worcestershire sauce, and poultry seasoning. Divide into 8 thick patties and press a 1-inch-deep hollow into each patty. Place them in a 13- by 9- by 2-inch pan. Bake in a preheated 375°F oven 15 minutes. Mix the catsup and water and spoon over the meat. Place the potato rounds in the hollows and continue baking 20 minutes. Remove the patties from the pan. Stir the pan juices to blend, adding water if necessary. Serve the sauce with the nests.

SERVES 8.

Ham Stroganoff with Rounds

    ½ cup minced onion
    ¼ cup butter
    ¼ cup flour
    1 can (6 ounces) sliced, broiled mush-
        rooms
    2 cups dairy sour cream
    1 pound cooked ham, cut into strips
    ½ teaspoon salt
      Dash pepper
    2 pounds frozen potato rounds

In a skillet, sauté the onion in the butter until tender. Add the flour and mix well. Add the mushrooms with the liquid from the can and the sour cream, blending well. Add the ham and salt and pepper and heat through. Prepare the potato rounds according to the directions on the package. Spoon the ham mixture over hot potato rounds.

SERVES 6 TO 8.

Crispy Potato Beef Hash

    1 pound ground beef
    1 tablespoon instant minced onion
    ½ cup chopped green pepper
    2 tablespoons peanut oil
    1 package (1 ounce) brown gravy mix
    ¾ cup water
    1 teaspoon salt
    ⅛ teaspoon pepper
    1 pound frozen potato rounds

Simmer the ground beef, onion, green pepper, and oil in a skillet until brown. Combine the gravy mix with the water and stir into the ground beef mixture. Season with salt and pepper and cook until slightly thickened. Turn the mixture into a 10- by 6- by 1½-inch baking dish. Arrange the potato rounds in a single layer on top. Bake in a preheated 425°F oven about 20 minutes until the potatoes are lightly browned.

SERVES 4.

Potato-Tomato Scallop

   2 cans (1 pound each) stewed tomatoes
   2 tablespoons flour
   1 tablespoon sugar
   1 teaspoon salt
  ⅛ teaspoon basil
  ⅛ teaspoon oregano
  ⅛ teaspoon pepper
   1 pound frozen potato rounds
  ¼ cup shredded cheddar cheese

Drain the tomatoes, reserving the liquid. In a medium-sized saucepan, combine the flour, sugar, and salt. Gradually add the tomato liquid, stirring until smooth. Add the tomatoes, basil, oregano, and pepper. Bring to a boil. Reduce the heat and simmer 5 minutes until thickened. Pour the mixture into a lightly greased 10-inch pie pan. Top with potato rounds and sprinkle with cheese. Bake in a preheated 350°F oven 25 minutes, until the potatoes are crisp and golden.

SERVES 5 TO 6.

Pizza Hashed Browns

1 package (12 ounces) frozen shredded
    hashed brown potatoes
Salad oil
Salt and pepper to taste
½ cup catsup or pizza sauce
½ cup grated mozzarella cheese

Arrange the potatoes in a single layer on a well-oiled shallow baking pan or cookie sheet. Brush the surface of the potatoes with oil. Sprinkle with salt and pepper. Bake, uncovered, 20 to 25 minutes in a preheated 500°F oven. Top with catsup or pizza sauce and sprinkle with cheese. Bake 5 to 10 minutes longer, until the potatoes are golden brown and the cheese is melted.

SERVES 4.

Crisp Potato Cakes

1 package (1 pound) shredded hashed
    brown potatoes, thawed and
    separated
⅓ cup grated onion
¼ cup flour
¼ cup dairy sour cream
3 eggs, slightly beaten
1¼ teaspoons salt
4 to 6 tablespoons lard

Combine the potatoes, onion, flour, sour cream, eggs, and salt. Heat the lard in a large frying pan. Drop the potato mixture (2 heaping teaspoons per cake) into the hot fat. With a spatula, flatten slightly to make 3-inch circles. Fry 4 to 5 minutes, until golden brown on both sides. Drain on paper towels.

MAKES ABOUT 16 CAKES.

Vegetable and Potato Patties

    1 package (9 ounces) frozen small onions
        with cream sauce, partly thawed
    ¾ cup water
    1 package (9 ounces) frozen cut green
        beans, partly thawed
    1 pound frozen shredded hashed brown
        potatoes
    1 package (10 ounces) frozen carrot
        nuggets in butter sauce, partly
        thawed.

Place the onions and cream sauce in the bottom of a 2-quart oblong baking dish. Pour the water over the onions. Spread the green beans over the onions. Separate the frozen potatoes into patties. Place the patties side by side on top of the green beans. Lift the carrots out of the butter sauce and arrange around the patties. Drizzle the butter sauce over the potatoes. Bake in a preheated 425°F oven 35 minutes, until the potatoes are fork-tender. Brown the potatoes under the broiler if desired.

SERVES 6.

Potato Dumplings

     2 cartons (12 ounces each) frozen shredded
          hashed brown potatoes
    ⅔ cup flour
     2 teaspoons salt
    ½ teaspoon nutmeg
    ¼ teaspoon pepper
     2 eggs, beaten

Thaw the hashed brown potatoes and separate the shreds with a fork. Combine the potatoes with the flour, salt, nutmeg, pepper, and eggs. Shape into balls and roll in extra flour. Drop into gently boiling stew or place on top of a pot roast. Cover and cook 15.to 20 minutes with the meat without removing the cover. When done, a wooden toothpick inserted in the center of the dumplings should come out clean.

MAKES 12 DUMPLINGS.

Pot of Gold Chowder

     2 tablespoons butter
    ½ onion, chopped
    ½ cup chopped celery
     2 cans (10 ounces each) frozen
          condensed oyster stew
     1 pound frozen fish fillets
    ½ pound frozen shrimp, peeled and
          deveined
     1 package (10 ounces) frozen succotash
    ¾ teaspoon salt
    ½ teaspoon pepper

1 quart milk, scalded
1 pound frozen southern-style hashed
    brown potatoes
6 slices bacon, cooked and crumbled
1 cup sharp natural cheddar cheese,
    shredded
¼ cup fresh parsley, chopped

In a 5-quart Dutch oven, melt the butter and sauté the onion and celery until tender. Add the oyster stew, fish fillets, shrimp, and succotash. Sprinkle the mixture with salt and pepper and pour the hot milk over all. Cover and simmer over a low heat 20 minutes, stirring occasionally. Stir in the frozen potatoes, cover, and simmer 15 minutes longer, until the potatoes are fork-tender. Serve garnished with bacon, cheese, and parsley.

SERVES 6 TO 8.

Hashed Browns in Wine

4 slices bacon, cut into pieces
½ cup butter
2 tablespoons chopped onion
1 pound frozen southern-style hashed
    brown potatoes
  Salt and pepper to taste
1 cup dry white wine

In a heavy saucepan, fry the bacon until cooked but not crisp. Add the butter and onion and continue cooking until the onion is golden. Stir in the frozen potatoes. Season with salt and pepper and add the wine. Cover and simmer 10 minutes, until the potatoes are fork-tender.

SERVES 3 TO 4.

Confetti Hashed Browns

¼ cup coarsely chopped green pepper
¼ cup sliced green onion
4 tablespoons salad oil
1 pound frozen southern-style hashed
    brown potatoes
½ teaspoon salt
½ teaspoon marjoram
  Dash pepper
1 small tomato, seeded and coarsely
    chopped

In a medium-sized frying pan, cook the green pepper and onion in 2 tablespoons of the salad oil. With a slotted spoon, remove the green pepper and onion from the pan and reserve. Add the remaining oil. Stir in the frozen potatoes, salt, marjoram, and pepper. Cook over a medium heat until the potatoes are tender and lightly browned. Add the green pepper, onion, and tomato and heat through, about 5 to 10 minutes.

SERVES 4.

Spicy Creamed Potatoes

1 pound frozen southern-style hashed
    brown potatoes
¾ cup boiling water
2 packages (1½ ounces each) white
    sauce mix
½ teaspoon Tabasco sauce
2 tablespoons chopped parsley
2 tablespoons chopped pimiento
3 tablespoons butter
½ cup soft bread crumbs
½ cup shredded sharp natural cheddar
    cheese
¼ teaspoon paprika

Add the hashed browns to the boiling water in a saucepan. Cover and simmer 10 minutes, until the potatoes are fork-tender, and drain. Prepare the sauce mix as directed on the package. Stir in the Tabasco sauce, parsley, pimiento, and cooked potatoes. Spoon into a 1½-quart casserole. Melt the butter in a small frying pan. Add the bread crumbs and toss to coat. Mix in the cheese and paprika. Sprinkle the crumbs around the edges of the casserole. Bake, uncovered, in a preheated 400°F oven 10 minutes, until the crumbs are lightly browned.

SERVES 6.

Dixie Hashed Browns

8 slices bacon
1 pound frozen southern-style hashed
   brown potatoes
½ teaspoon salt
½ teaspoon poultry seasoning

In a medium-sized frying pan, cook the bacon until crisp. Remove and drain. Add the frozen potatoes to the bacon fat and sprinkle with salt and poultry seasoning. Cook over a medium heat, stirring occasionally, until the potatoes are tender and lightly browned. Crumble the bacon over the potatoes and serve.

SERVES 4.

Crunchy Hashed Browns

1 medium-sized onion, grated
¼ cup enriched yellow corn meal
   Salt and pepper to taste
1 pound frozen southern-style hashed
   brown potatoes
¾ cup vegetable oil

In a large bowl, combine the onion, corn meal, salt, and pepper. Add the frozen potatoes and mix well. In a medium-sized frying pan, heat the vegetable oil. Add the potato mixture and cook until golden brown and crusty, stirring frequently.

SERVES 4.

Tart and Tangy Potato Salad

½ cup cider vinegar
⅓ cup water
½ teaspoon seasoned salt
⅛ teaspoon seasoned pepper
2 tablespoons sugar
1 pound frozen southern-style hashed
    brown potatoes
⅓ cup mayonnaise
½ cup celery, finely chopped
1 green onion, thinly sliced
2 large radishes, thinly sliced
¼ large cucumber, unpeeled and very
    thinly sliced
Salad greens
5 bacon slices, crisply cooked and
    crumbled
3 hard-cooked eggs, sliced

In a medium-sized saucepan, combine the vinegar, water, salt, pepper, and sugar and heat to a boil. Stir in the potatoes, cover, and simmer until the potatoes are tender, about 5 minutes. Cool slightly. Lightly toss the potatoes with the mayonnaise and vegetables. Serve warm or cold on salad greens. Garnish with bacon bits and sliced eggs. For a less tangy salad, substitute ½ cup water and ⅓ cup vinegar for the proportions listed.

SERVES 6.

Tara 'Taters

      2 pounds southern-style hashed brown
            potatoes, partly thawed
      ¼ cup coarsely chopped green pepper
      1 jar (2 ounces) sliced pimientos, drained
            and chopped
      2 cups milk
   1 ¼ teaspoons salt
      ¾ cup fine dry bread crumbs
      ⅓ cup soft butter
      ⅔ cup sharp processed cheddar cheese,
            shredded

Put the potatoes into a greased 2-quart baking dish, separating the pieces. Add the green pepper and pimientos and mix lightly. Combine the milk and salt and pour over the potatoes. Cover with foil. Bake in a preheated 350°F oven 1¼ hours, until the potatoes are fork-tender. Remove the foil and top with a mixture of bread crumbs, butter, and cheese. Continue baking 15 minutes, until the cheese is melted.

SERVES 6.

Index